Green's Filing Systems

Green's Filing Systems

For Pastors and Christian Workers

Michael P. Green

BAKER BOOK HOUSE
Grand Rapids, Michigan

Published in the United States of America.

Library of Congress Cataloging-in-Publication Data

Green, Michael P.
    [Filing systems for pastors and Christian workers]
    Green's filing systems for pastors and Christian workers / by Michael P. Green.
        p.   cm.
    ISBN 0-8010-3846-4
    1. Filing systems. 2. Church records and registers—Handbooks, manuals, etc.   I. Title. II. Title: Filing systems for pastors and Christian workers.
BV4379.G69   1991
651.4'042—dc20
                                            91-15117
                                                 CIP

The Student's Lament

Ram it in!
Cram it in!
Student's heads are hollow!

Slam it in!
Jam it in!
Still there's more to follow!

The Minister's Lament

I rammed it in.
I crammed it in.
Now I am much older.

I slammed it in.
I jammed it in.
Why can't I find that folder?

Contents

**Part 2: Sample
Filing Systems**

Preface

This work is written for those who have never found the time and discipline to organize their information as well as for those who have a filing system that is more of a burden than a servant to them and their ministry.

Filing is usually considered to be something best put off until later on. If you have never been filled with visions of everything neatly organized, then this book is for you!

People, not filing systems, go to heaven. Extra time spent filing material is wasted. Extra time spent finding material is wasted. Thus the goal of filing.

For Whom Was This Book Written?

Is Filing Worth the Effort?

The goal of any filing system should be to minimize time spent filing and finding materials so as to maximize time for ministry.

Overview

This book was written with the intention to make using it as easy as possible. So how should it be used?

First, read this overview and chapter 1. You will then know what this book is trying to accomplish.

Second, pay attention to the first paragraph of each chapter titled Overview. It will give you the questions that chapter will answer. Keep them in mind as you read.

Third, skim the headings in the wide margins before you begin to gain an overview of the chapter's structure.

Fourth, use the wide margins for your personal notes.

After you read this overview and chapter 1, if you are sure what kind of filing system you want, read either chapter 2 or 3, whichever applies. If you aren't sure which system is for you, read both chapters 2 and 3 and spend a few minutes going over chapters 8 and 9 to see how these two approaches to filing look in practice.

Chapters 4, 5, and 6 deal with specific filing problems and can be skipped at first. However, chapter 7 is full of great ideas that you'll want to know when you actually start your filing system so be sure to read it.

The following paragraphs will give you a quick overview of the entire book.

Chapter 1 discusses what to file and examines three criteria or requirements that are characteristic of all effective filing systems. A survey of the two basic approaches to filing concludes the chapter.

Chapter 2 describes the approach to filing that uses an index book. These filing systems locate material in folders under either a numerical or alphabetical scheme. Chapter 8 is a sample of this type of filing system.

Chapter 3 describes the second widely used approach to filing: using topics and subtopics. Systems built on this approach rely on the principle of subordination (or outlining) for organization. They are thus self-indexing and do not use an index book. Chapter 9 is a sample of this type of filing system.

How to Use This Book

Can I Skip Anything?

Overview

(Chapters 4, 5, and 6 apply to both approaches to filing and may be read independently of chapters 1, 2, and 3.)

Chapter 4 presents an easy to use system for filing material related to the books of the Bible. Chapter 10 is a sample of this type of filing system.

Chapter 5 examines several ways of filing sermons, messages, and Bible studies. A simple and effective method is recommended. In addition, the problem of finding research done on a Bible passage or topic which is filed somewhere other than under the passage is dealt with. The solution hinges on developing an indexing system. A simple-to-use indexing system is described.

Chapter 6 discusses principles for the filing of narrative illustrative material on index cards or on a computer data base.

Chapter 7 is a collection of ideas and suggestions for effective filing. It should be read by everyone.

Chapters 8 and 9 present a sample filing system for those in Christian ministry. The system is organized as a separately indexed system in chapter 8 and as a topic-subtopic system in chapter 9.

Chapter 10 presents the structure of the Bible filing system described in chapter 4.

Chapter 11 presents a suggested list of topics for filing illustrations.

The appendix is in the form of a suggested class assignment for a filing system. It concludes with a grade sheet.

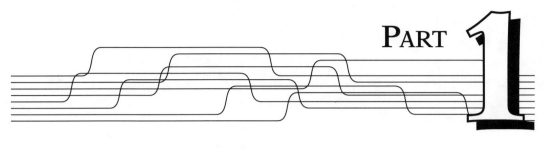

PART 1

Principles
of Filing

An Effective Filing System

This chapter will answer the following questions:

Overview

• What items should be filed?
• What are the traits of a good filing system?
• What basic strategies or approaches to filing should I consider?
• What are the strengths and weaknesses of each basic strategy?

What Should You File?

File all articles, notes, papers, sermons, and other materials relating to the following.

File Materials Relating to:

Materials relating to ministry subjects that you or someone in your church or ministry might need should be filed. For example:

Ministry subjects

a handout on ideas for what to say when making a hospital visitation,
a job description for a DVBS coordinator, or
contact charts for an evangelistic outreach.

Those who also work in another vocation will need to file materials related to their job or profession.

Bible study materials that you might have use for when studying a passage or preparing a message or sermon should be filed. For example:

Bible passages

an article that gives helpful details of the role of geography in an Old Testament battle,
an A+ paper done by a friend in school, or
notes from a class you took in school.

Sermons, messages, and Bible studies

Every sermon, message, and Bible study you develop should be filed. Some prefer to place these in a separate section. Others file them under the appropriate topic or Bible passage. Indexing these materials is often as important as filing them.

Correspondence

Correspondence should be filed. Casual personal correspondence often is not saved, but those in ministry often treasure it in their later years. Letters to you and your replies have a way of becoming extremely important just after they were thrown out! Correspondence that is job related should be filed for future reference.

Other materials

Other kinds of materials that you might need in the future should be filed. For example:

a file for each year at school or in a ministry containing pictures and other remembrances,
your resumé,
theological issues,
tax records.

Illustrations

Illustrations are essential to effective communication and thus need to be filed. Many file their illustrations on 3x5 or 4x6 cards. Others use a computer data base for storing illustrative material.

Before we examine the actual process of developing a filing system and how to pick a system that will be best for you, we will look at three criteria or requirements for an effective filing system.

Three Requirements for an Effective Filing System

Simple

A filing system should be simple to set up, maintain, and use. It should not require a user to be a workaholic or organizational genius. It should save time in locating materials. Others should be able to understand it quickly and to such an extent that they can find and file materials when necessary.

Consistent

Many items potentially can be filed under several different headings. A consistent system will always use the same file heading for the same category of information. This trait of consistency should be designed into the system. The very architecture or design of the system should reflect and encourage consistency as the system develops.

In a well-designed city, the street system will enable people to get to their desired destination quickly without confusion or inefficiency. A consistent filing system does the same thing. It enables users to find desired information quickly without taking them to wrong categories or causing them to be uncertain that they are on the right path.

The implementation of consistency is particularly difficult when dealing with *related* topics. For example, the material from a seminar on evangelism could be filed under several different headings such as: Evangelism, Soteriology, Soul Winning, or Witnessing. It matters little which one is used but, *which one will* be used? How will that decision be made?

A second and perhaps even more difficult question to answer is "How can I be sure that in four or five years I will be able to recall where this material was filed without looking through several file drawers?" What in the system insures that the user will not deviate from the previously established list of file categories? This is particularly important for students and young ministers whose categories for filing will undergo major change as the language of theology and ministry is adopted. In addition many areas of ministry change name over time. For example in the 1950s most books on evangelism had "soul winning" in their title, but by the 1980s the term had nearly disappeared in favor of terms such as *evangelism*, *friendship evangelism*, and so forth. A similar change was the 1960s and 70s "social issues" that by the 1980s were referred to as "ethical issues."

An effective system will *by its design* solve these two problems of maintaining consistent headings.

Flexible

Since life always involves change, present interests and needs, especially for students, will be different from what future interests will be as a pastor, teacher, missionary, or other minister. Therefore, a filing system should be flexible enough to change as needs change. A flexible system will have the following three characteristics.

Ability to expand

A good filing system can *expand* into new areas of interest without distorting the rest of the file system.

For example, perhaps you were the children's minister in your church and now have become the senior pastor. As senior pastor there are many areas of ministry for which you will need to file materials that previously you never thought of. Such areas could be records of meetings and plans for various church boards, ideas for and records of worship services, sermons, building programs, and so forth. Your system should be able to quickly and easily expand to pick up these new areas.

Ability to contract

A second trait of a flexible filing system is the ability to *contract* or allow you to remove and store files that are no longer used or needed. This is necessary because as a ministry develops and changes, materials that once were used frequently will no longer be needed.

For an example we will continue with the previous illustration of you as the former children's minister who has just become the senior pastor. While children's ministries are still important to you and to the church, you probably do not need two or three file drawers of children's ministry materials at your fingertips in your office file cabinet. Indeed to keep them there probably will mean buying another file cabinet and then figuring out where to put it! Therefore, your file system should allow you to contract or remove the unused files for disposal or storage. Then you will not find yourself forced to keep a large number of unused file folders in your file cabinet. At the same time your filing system should have the flexibility to retrieve and reintegrate the files into your system if at sometime in the future you find the need for frequent access to them.

Ability to be detailed or general

A third trait of a flexible filing system is the ability to *be detailed or general* in different areas. The level of detail in each major heading or area should not be tied to the level of detail in other areas.

For example, in your Bible file for Genesis you may have all of your materials for a Sunday school class. This will require a considerable number of folders to be properly organized. However, if you never taught Exodus you should be able to have just one folder for Exodus next to the many folders for Genesis.

Summary

In summary, a filing system should be simple to set up, maintain, and use, consistent in where materials are filed, and flexible enough to expand, contract, and be detailed or general as is needed.

The Two Basic Solutions to These Requirements

The scores of published filing systems can be reduced to two types or approaches. These are *separately indexed systems* and *topic-subtopic systems*.

Role of Personality

The individual who is about to begin the labor intensive process of organizing a filing system should first decide which of these two basic approaches to use. While most proponents of an approach are zealous that theirs is best, the true "best" system is the one that works for you because it helps you in your ministry. Thus, personal preference (personality, style of ministry, and so forth) should be the primary factor in choosing a basic approach. It unquestionably will be the primary factor in shaping the system and in determining its usefulness.

The following two chapters describe these two approaches. Read both chapters before deciding which system to use. Although most people want to begin the process of developing a filing system as soon as possible, to do so without a full understanding of how the basic approach works is to multiply the time needed to complete the task.

Chart 1 summarizes how the three criteria for an effective filing system apply to the two basic approaches to filing. (The comments in the chart are more fully developed in the next two chapters.)

Chart 1
Comparison of Filing Systems

Criteria	Separately Indexed Systems	Topic-Subtopic Systems
Simplicity	Initial: development of topics and cross-references requires detailed work, is difficult, and time consuming.	Initial: development of topics and subtopics requires independent thought, is difficult, and time consuming.
	Ongoing: extreme ease of use because system uses an index book. However, use of the index book adds an extra step to the retrieval process.	Ongoing: variable ease of use (from moderate to easy), dependent on the care given to initial development.
	New user needs to learn only how to use the index book to use the system.	New user must learn the basic structure of the system before using.
Consistency	Index book guarantees consistency if all synonymous headings and all related topics have been thoroughly cross-referenced.	Subordination of all topics under a few major topics automatically leads the user to the general area in the file system where the material will be located.
Flexibility	Easy to add new files if the index book has room for additional topics.	Extremely easy to add or remove files as needed.
	Difficult to remove all related files without going through every listing in the index book. Numerical systems are very difficult to contract.	

Separately Indexed Filing Systems

This chapter will answer the following questions:

- What is a separately indexed filing system, how does it file materials, and what type of personality likes this approach?
- How does this kind of filing system meet the criteria of simplicity, consistency, and flexibility?
- Why is it so important to have cross-referencing in the index book?
- How can a separately indexed filing system be made?

Introduction

Description— An Indexing Approach to Filing

A separately indexed filing system is one that uses an index book to list the hundreds of categories (topics, headings, file-folder titles) used in the filing system. The topics are listed alphabetically in the book with little or no subordination. Materials may be filed in alphabetical order[1] or according to a numbering scheme like the one a library uses to shelve books.

Separately indexed

To file or retrieve material, the user must first go to the index book to find the category under which the material was filed. This step is faster than opening and closing several file drawers to look for an elusive folder. For example, although meaning basically the same thing, materials could be filed under *E* for evangelism, *S* for soul-winning, or *W* for witnessing. To look through several file drawers is much more time consuming than looking through an index book.

Filed in alphabetical or numerical order

Filing systems that use an index book place file folders in file drawers in either alphabetical or numerical order.

Systems filing in alphabetical order require the user to place a mark in the index book next to the heading to be used

---

1. Sometimes an ordering other than alphabetical may be desirable. For example, chronological order for history and canonical order for Bible books.

for a new folder. If the desired heading isn't in the index book, it is written into the book. The mark or handwritten entry shows that a folder exists for that heading. Then the user prepares a folder with that heading on it and files it.

Systems filing in numerical order assign a number to each folder. This number is either based on chronological sequence (the first folder made is #1, the second is #2, and so forth) or on a numerical scheme worked out in advance (like the catalog numbers a library uses for indexing books). If the index number is not preassigned in the index book, it is written in the index book next to the heading so that the user can find the folder. The number is then written on the folder and it is filed in numerical order.

Effectiveness

A separately indexed filing system has some potential advantages and weaknesses. The following discussion examines separately indexed filing systems based on the three criteria of simplicity, consistency, and flexibility.

Simplicity

Since the filing categories are thought through only once (when the system is constructed), separately indexed systems save the user a great deal of time in daily use. Since the headings are in a book it is easy to show someone else how to use the filing system. Thus the index book feature of the separately indexed system fulfills the requirement of simplicity.

Consistency

The use of an index book allows separately indexed filing systems to have the potential for a high level of consistency. However, this is where the potential weakness of such a system is most evident.

Cross-referencing solves problems of synonymous and related headings

The separately indexed approach to filing must deal with the problems of synonymous headings and related headings. Fortunately both problems are solved with the same solution—cross-referencing.

Synonymous headings

Synonymous headings are those that are basically covering the same topic. Usually the difference between synonymous headings is a minor nuance that many users won't pick up. For example the following three headings refer to the same topic: Evangelism, Soul Winning, and Witnessing. Which one will you use? How will you be sure that in the future you don't begin to use another one of these three synonymous headings and so lose access to materials filed under the other? How will you ensure that a secretary or other person filing for you will use the correct heading?

This problem is not theoretical. One published system has three different headings under which material on the parables can be filed. A secretary might file an article under the first heading "Bible, Parables," while you use the third "Parables." Unless you happened to notice the duplication in the index the first article would be irretrievable because you're looking in the "Ps" while it's filed in the "Bs" (The third heading is "Christ, Parables"). The difference between these three headings is elusive at best. The point is that all separately indexed filing systems are open to the same kind of loss of consistency.

Extensive and carefully thought-out cross-referencing is the best solution to this problem. To be effective, cross-referencing should be added when a new heading is added to the system. Computer word-processing programs have made this task much easier. (See the section in chapter 6 on Computers.)

Related headings

Even when materials are filed under the correct heading, there may be related materials filed under other headings. For example material that might be useful for a message on counseling might be in the "Counseling" folder (a subject found in the index book). But there also might be folders titled "Worry" and "Anxiety" that contain materials helpful for a message on counseling. How will the user be alerted to the existence of these materials?

The solution to this problem is additional cross-referencing. In this case, the index book should have cross-references between the file folders labeled "Counseling," "Worry," and "Anxiety."

Flexibility

If the user can choose not to use certain titles and can write in additional titles in the index book, then a separately indexed filing system is flexible.

To be truly flexible, the index book must have room for additional headings to be added. If the index book does not have such capacity, then the user will either not make up a new folder when needed or try to scribble the new title in the margin of the index book. Neither is conducive to easy filing and easy retrieval of materials. A user of this approach to filing should, as a rule of thumb, leave space in the index book for three to five additional titles between each original title.

The user who plans to develop an index book may wish to use a blank bound book. A sturdy binding will prevent the loss of pages, and the book form makes it easy to shelve.

If loose leaf paper and a three ring binder are to be used, it is wise to purchase heavy weight paper with a reinforced edge. This paper will last considerably longer under daily use and is worth the extra cost.

Those developing their index on a computer may leave only

one or two additional lines between titles since they can easily update their list and print out a new index.

Personality Factor

What type of personality prefers the separately indexed approach? Typically the person who is a particularist more than a generalist, who is more of an analytical thinker than a synthetic thinker. If you are the kind of person who "likes his ducks all lined up in a neat row," who tends to think of things just as they are rather than as a part of a larger concept or framework, then this may be the approach for you.

Constructing a Separately Indexed Filing System

The following suggestions may be helpful for constructing a separately indexed filing system.

Obtain examples of several model systems

If possible, obtain several lists of other systems used by those in a ministry similar to yours, or one that you hope to have in the future. These will give you ideas for topics/titles to use and help you to see what topics need cross-referencing. (See chapter 7 for a sample separately indexed filing system.)

Carefully plan your system

Decide if you will file your materials in alphabetical order or according to a numerical scheme such as the library uses. If you decide to use a published separately indexed filing system, this decision will be made for you.

If you decide to file your materials in alphabetical order, consider these suggestions. When first constructing your system, begin by marking several sheets of paper for each letter of the alphabet. Use these sheets to construct your system. As you write in topics, leave lots of blank lines so that you can add topics later. A computer word-processing program that has the function of sorting by letter of the alphabet can be extremely useful for composing a separately indexed filing system. It allows the user to type in items randomly and let the computer sort them into alphabetical order.

If you decide to file your materials based on a separately indexed approach, consider a published one. Several popular published systems are available.[2]

2. *New Baker's Textual and Topical Filing System*, prepared by Neal Punt (1989), is a large oversized index book. The book contains three sections: topical index, textual index, and references spaces. The topical index has twenty-two hundred topics to use for filing materials, is cross-indexed for synonyms, antonyms, and related topics, and provides space between each topic for additional topics. The textual index provides space, under each book of the Bible, for listing commentaries and materials for each chapter of that book. The reference spaces are two thousand quarter page sections with twenty lines for recording the materials filed under that reference number. Folders are numbered in chronological sequence with the number being noted in the topical index and the contents listed in the reference space under that number. Of course, the same thing can be done by purchasing a blank book and using it in the manner described. Although not a system for procrastinators, Punt's topical index is well done and the cross-indexing is carefully thought out.

The *Rossin-Dewey Subject List* (R-DSL), published by The Shepherd Company, is based on the Dewey Decimal

Users of separately indexed systems often wonder what to do with the three tabs on file folders. Many do not realize that the folder tabs can help to make the basic structure of a system clear and thus increase its effectiveness.

Using folder tabs to help clarify your system's structure

Some users of alphabetical order systems simply file items in the sequence left tab, middle tab, right tab, etc. The problem with this method is that when additional folders are placed in the system, they will destroy the left-middle-right order of the system. File all topics that begin with the same letter in a folder using the same tab cut. The following chart illustrates this.

Using tabs in an alphabetical order system

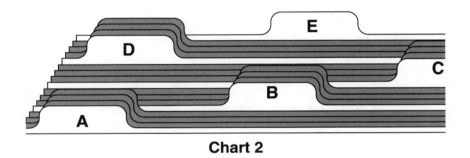

Chart 2

Users of numerical order systems also often wonder what to do with the three tabs on file folders. Some simply use whatever comes up next. There is an easier way to use the system in the long run. If the files are in a numerical order based on chronology (the first folder created is #1, the second is #2, and so on) then use the three cuts in the sequence left-middle-right. This will insure that two folders come between folders of the same tab and thus should make the tab more visible. The following chart illustrates this.

Using tabs in a numerical order system

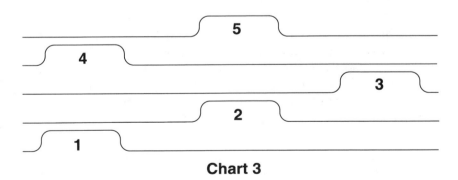

Chart 3

Classification System (DDC), which is widely used in libraries. The user of this system simply labels and files the file folders in the system according to the numbering given in the R-DSL booklet. This system is difficult to classify because when put into a file cabinet it looks like a topic-subtopic system, but in use and format it is a separately indexed system. The R-DSL has "over 2200 alphabetically arranged titles or subjects in religion, psychology, and social science; each with the official Dewey or a suggested numerical classification number."

If the files are in a numerical order based on a system such as the one the library uses, then it is better to let the tabs reflect the system. One tab should be used for all of the folders at each level of the system such as tens or hundreds. The following chart illustrates this.

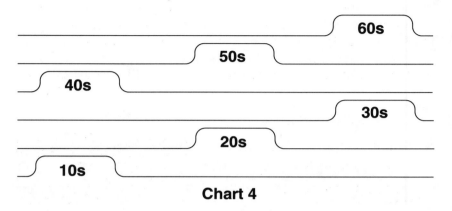

Chart 4

Adding folders as a system matures

As a folder begins to accumulate more and more material, it will become too thick to use easily and quickly. When this happens, the contents of the folder should be divided into several narrower topics or folders. Often these will be the original folder's name with an added comma and subcategory. For example, a folder on "ABC Mission" may expand to become three folders: "ABC, History"; "ABC, Finances"; and "ABC, Missionaries."

Books of the Bible Files

Materials relating to the Bible are best filed in the system described in chapter 4. That chapter and chapter 10 should be read before the Bible section of your filing system is constructed. Note that the order for the Bible files is canonical, not alphabetical.

Dividing Up the System into Separate Files

Many users of separately indexed systems keep part of their file at home and part at work. This can be indicated in the index book by use of a code such as *H* for those folders kept at home. To save time and effort, do not code the location where most of the folders are kept. In other words, the *H* code would tell the user that the file is somewhere other than where most of the files are.

Topic-Subtopic Filing Systems

3

Overview

This chapter will answer the following questions:

- What is a topic-subtopic filing system, how does it file material, and what type of personality likes this approach?
- How does this kind of filing system meet the criteria of simplicity, consistency, and flexibility?
- How can a topic-subtopic filing system be made?

Introduction

**Description—
An Outlining
Approach**

The second major approach to filing is an outlining approach using topics and subtopics. A topic is a broad category of information. A subtopic is a narrower category of information. All subtopics are subordinate to and directly related to a broader category of information (a topic). Filing systems using this approach file material under specific headings that are filed under broader headings.

In other words, topic-subtopic filing systems file materials in folders based on a logically developed outline using extensive subordination of topics. This synthetic approach is in contrast to the approach of using an alphabetical listing of topics in an index book (the separately indexed approach). Although an index can be made, topic-subtopic filing systems are usually self-indexing.

Structure

The structure of a topic-subtopic or outline filing system is based on the three cuts or tabs that standard file folders have (left tab, middle tab, right tab). The organization of a filing system and its correspondence to an outline system are diagrammed in the chart that follows. Note that the file drawer is the broadest level of organization. Thus there are as many as four levels of organization available to the user.

Chart 5

Organi- zational level	Broadest category (Level one)	Broad category (Level two)	Narrow category (Level three)	Narrowest category (Level four)
Outline indicator	I (Roman numerals)	A (Upper case letters)	1 (Arabic numerals)	a (Lower case letters)
Filing indicator	File drawer	Left cut/tab	Middle cut/tab	Right cut/tab

Weakness

Topic-subtopic systems are based on an outlined organization of the topics needing filing. An outline is a synthetic way of organizing information. Since there are many ways to synthesize information, the most effective outline is one the user has created. Therefore, the importance of carefully and clearly thinking through which broad categories the system will be built on cannot be overstated. Simplicity, consistency, and flexibility are possible only if careful thought is given to the development of major or broad headings and subheadings.

Strength

Once a topic-subtopic system has been worked out and set up, it is very difficult to misplace materials because they are filed where the user would logically think of them. In other words, since your "logic" or way of thinking was the basis for the topics and subtopics used, you will nearly always be able to find what you want either by simply thinking it through or by backing up to a broader category and visually scanning down through the folders under that category. An index can be typed to assist you in this, if desired, but is not necessary.

Effectiveness

A topic-subtopic filing system has some potential advantages and weaknesses compared to a separately indexed filing system. The following discussion examines topic-subtopic filing systems based on the three criteria of simplicity, consistency, and flexibility.

Simplicity

The major weakness of the topic-subtopic approach is the initial work involved in developing the system. A second difficulty occurs whenever the user has to teach someone else, such as a secretary, how to use the system. It will take time for a new user to understand the system's organization. This is a serious disadvantage only if people who will be expected to use the system will not do so long enough to master its basic structure.

A topic-subtopic system can be extremely consistent if it is constructed on a stable framework. The user must be very consistent at the level of broad category and not have two broad categories for filing the same information. To do so results in a filing system best described as chaotic.

The specific heading under which something is filed is often somewhat arbitrary. This was discussed in the previous chapter as the problems of synonymous and related headings. Separately indexed filing systems solve these problems by using extensive cross-referencing in the index book.

Topic-subtopic filing systems use a different strategy to solve these problems. They do not require the user to be able to recall the specific heading. Instead users go to the broad category of information they are interested in and begin to think their way down to the level of a specific heading or category.

The problem of using synonymous terms to describe the same topic is not directly solved. In a topic-subtopic system, the final place in which a folder can be, regardless of which synonymous term was used for filing, is usually contained within a few inches from the first spot checked, a space the eye can easily skim over to locate the correct folder.

Subordination of ideas—the heart of outlining—automatically places all related topics near each other. In this manner a topic-subtopic filing system solves the problem of related headings.

The problems of synonymous and related headings are solved through the use of subordination of ideas

For example, all materials concerning spiritual gifts should be filed together. The difficulty is where to put them—in the "Theology" section under "Pneumatology" (the doctrine of the Holy Spirit) or under "Ecclesiology" (the doctrine of the church)? Or, if your orientation is less theological and more practical, then perhaps a category such as "Ministry" would be best. *The point is that only one category should exist in a topic-subtopic system under which specific material is filed, otherwise the system will not be consistent.* Once that one category has been established, a topic-subtopic system automatically places all of your materials on spiritual gifts next to each other.

Let's assume you choose to file your materials on spiritual gifts under the category of "Theology." This will be either a file drawer heading or a left cut file folder. As you go to the "Theology" file drawer heading or left cut folder, you think of a more specific category, in this case "Pneumatology." This will be one level in or to the right from Theology (that is, a left or middle cut folder depending on where Theology is). Then, since Pneumatology is still too broad, you would go to an even more specific subtopic such as "Gifts, Seminar notes" (a middle or right cut folder). If you do not think of the Holy Spirit under the heading of Pneumatology you could file your materials under "Holy Spirit." It would make little difference in use because the actual space between where a Holy Spirit folder and a Pneumatology folder would be in the Theology section usually would not be more than a few inches—a space your eyes could easily jump over or scan across. Note that files under (that is, to the right of) any broader file or category are filed alphabetically within that subcategory. (If this is not clear, take a few minutes now to look over chapter 9.)

Special challenges to consistency in a topic-subtopic filing system

An additional difficulty with topic-subtopic filing systems is that there are some areas of information that are related and yet end up filed from the beginning to the end of the file system. An example is topics such as racism, abortion, poverty programs, human rights, pornography, right to die with dignity, pollution, and so forth. Resource materials that you collect on these topics will often deal with several of these issues in one article. Answers that you develop for one of these issues will often apply to others. The solution to this problem that maintains consistency is to recognize that all of these are related as social or ethical issues. Thus, they should all be filed under a broad category such as "Ethics" or "Social Issues."

A similar problem arises with topics such as singleness, dating, marriage, childrearing, and so forth. These areas are so interrelated that much of the material filed under one would apply to another. For example, material developed for a high school seminar on why students should exercise moral self-discipline before marriage will be appropriate for premarital counseling and even for certain marital counseling situations. One solution is to recognize the relatedness of these topics as belonging to the category of "Christian Home" or perhaps "Counseling." The principle is that materials that are broadly related are best filed together.

Flexibility

Topic-subtopic systems are very flexible. They can expand with no more effort than making up additional file folders and possibly moving a few folders down to the next drawer to give extra room for the new folders. Topic-subtopic filing systems can contract by simply removing the unneeded folders to a storage box or waste basket. The only requirement is that *all* folders or tabs to the right (or "under") the folder to be removed also must be removed.

Personality Factor

What type of personality prefers the topic-subtopic approach? Typically, the person who is more of a generalist than a particularist, more of a synthetic thinker than an analytical thinker. If you are the kind of person who can see the forest from the trees, who thinks in terms of broad categories or concepts, who is more concerned about "the big picture" than the particulars, then this may be the approach that will work best for you.

Constructing a Topic-Subtopic Filing System

When constructing a self-indexing, topic-subtopic system the following suggestions may be helpful.

Suggestions

If possible, obtain several lists of other systems used by those in a ministry similar to yours, or that you hope to have in the future. These will give you ideas for topics/titles to use and help you to see what topics logically subordinate themselves under broader topics. See chapter 9 for a sample topic-subtopic filing system.

Obtain examples of several model systems

To write out your system, begin by drawing two lines down several sheets of paper to make three columns. Use these sheets to construct your system. The three columns on the paper correspond to the three cuts on your file folders or to three levels of indentation in an outline. As you write in topics, leave lots of blank lines so that you can add additional topics later.

Carefully plan your system

Chart 6

Sample Page Used for Developing a Topic-Subtopic Filing System

Audio Visuals		
	Catalogs	
		Films
		Tapes
	Committee Equipment Manuals	
		Movie Projector
		Slide Projector
		VCR
	Graphics Overhead Masters	
		Bible Geography
		Life of Christ
	Slide Library Index Tape Library Index	
Baby Dedication		
	Ceremony	

The essential element of a topic-subtopic system is the ability to subordinate material. Therefore, in the topic-subtopic approach the user needs to ensure that he or she will be able

Gaining an additional level of subordination

to subordinate sufficiently. An additional or fourth level of outline may be needed for major topics that will literally fill one or more drawers with subordinate subtopics. The solution to this is simple. The file drawer itself can be considered to be another level of the outline. Thus, four levels of outline can be used by adding the file drawer itself as part of your outline. Experience has shown that four levels are sufficient to organize nearly anything.

In the inital stage of developing a topic-subtopic file system the user should seek to anticipate those broad categories that will likely need all three levels of subordination provided by standard third cut folders. The broadest topics should be typed on a slip of paper and placed in the rectangular bracket on the drawer.

A discussion of areas that are likely candidates for being a broadest category will occur later. Such broadest categories can be indicated on your worksheet by use of another color of ink. When first developing a topic-subtopic filing system, it is best to try to limit the number of broadest categories to fewer than ten. Many excellent filing systems have only three or four broadest categories.

When beginning a filing system, most of your broadest categories will not have much material. Setting a whole file drawer aside for a few folders may seem wasteful. The solution is to recognize that one file drawer can accommodate more than one broadest topic. The cardboard back of a pad can be cut to fit and used as a divider between the broadest categories in a single file drawer. Or, stationery stores sell dividers for this purpose.

Broadest categories (file drawers) commonly needed when using the topic-subtopic approach

Topics which will be so broad that they will need a fourth level of outline are those in which you anticipate needing more ability to subordinate than just middle and right cuts would provide. This situation commonly occurs in the categories of Bible, Messages, Ministry, Personal, and Theology. A section called "General" can be used for everything else.

Anticipating the need for additional subordination in the design stage of a topic-subtopic filing system is imperative if the user wishes to avoid the laborious task of reorganization later on. Users who are just beginning to build their file system probably will not have a full file drawer of material and thus may be tempted not to identify and plan for these broadest areas. A good filing system will seek to anticipate these areas and incorporate them into its system from the start. Initially, this may mean that several of these broadest categories will be in a single drawer.

As a particular folder begins to accumulate more and more material it will become too thick to use easily and quickly. When this happens, the contents of the folder should be divided into several narrower categories or folders.

When a system is first set up, the user may be able to anticipate some of the categories that will expand in the future. In such cases, simply go ahead and prepare those folders.

As a topic-subtopic system becomes more developed, some folders may be empty because all of the material is filed in subordinate folders under (to the right of) the empty folder. In this case, the broad folder is simply functioning as a place marker. This is not to be deplored as wasteful because the purpose of the system is to enable you to minimize time spent filing and finding materials so as to maximize ministry time. An empty folder, which only costs a few pennies is a small price to pay for helping you accomplish your goal!

Sometimes these place marker folders will be used to hold material of a broad or survey nature for that topic. For example, in a file system under the left cut folder labeled "Colleges" will be center cut folders for various schools. Under the center cut folder labeled with the name of the college you attended, there might be a right cut folder for each year at that school. Thus, it would seem that the left cut folder "Colleges" may be an empty or place-marker folder. However, it may contain a brochure titled "How to Pick a College" and several related articles.

Adding folders as a system matures

Materials relating to the Bible are best filed in the system described in chapter 4. That chapter and chapter 10 should be read before the Bible section of your filing system is constructed.

Books of the Bible Files

An administration or ministry section includes all of the materials used in a ministry or job. In the case of a pastor the broadest topic is usually "Church Administration," "Christian Education," or something similar.

Administration or Ministry Files

The reason for this section is purely pragmatic—it is easier! For example, when preparing a new job description for a Sunday school teacher, it is often helpful to look at the job descriptions for several other positions for ideas. If all of your job descriptions are filed near each other, this is easy to do. An additional benefit of having all of your job-related files in one section is that others who might need to have specific ministry materials will not be looking through your entire file system to find them.

In the case of those who are not in vocational Christian work, there may still be a need for ministry categories. In addition, they probably will need to make their vocational area a broadest category.

**Correspon-
dence**

For some, correspondence will become a significant aspect of their work. For most, it will not be necessary to make this into a separate broadest category in their file. Correspondence can be filed by date (chronological order), state (geographical order), addressee (alphabetical order), or by topic. It is often essential to file copies of important correspondence and copies of personal letters are often treasured in one's later years of ministry.

Theology

Many students and ministers "think theologically," that is, in theological categories. Their "Theology" section tends to become large and is thus a good candidate for making into a broadest category or file drawer. Ministerial students are encouraged to give serious consideration to making Theology into a broadest category.

Since no two theologians use the same organizational structure and the same vocabulary (nomenclature), how should the theology section be organized? Perhaps the most functional solution is simply to use the system of your favorite theologian for both organizational structure and nomenclature.

Personal

Many individuals have extensive personal files covering taxes, budgets, family members, and so forth, and thus need an extra level of subordination and physical closeness. In addition, by placing all of your personal files together under a broadest heading of "Personal," they can be kept at home and not in your office, where they are accessible to people who have no need to see them.

Filing Bible-Related Materials

This chapter will answer the following questions:

Overview

• What is an easy way to file Bible-related material in a simple, consistent, and flexible manner?
• How should I file material from the Gospels where there is so much overlap of content between four distinct books?
• How should I file word studies, survey material, and other Bible-related items?

Introduction

Usefulness

The following system for filing Bible materials is so simple, consistent, easy-to-use, and flexible that most individuals adopt it for their Bible files regardless of the type of filing system used for other materials.

Basic Organization

Left tab folders are used for each book, middle tabs for major divisions of the book, and right tabs for teaching or preaching units. Initially sixty-six left tab folders will meet your needs, one for each book of the Bible. Middle and right tab folders can be added whenever needed. The divisions to use for your middle tabs can come from a survey of several commentaries in which you look for agreement on major divisions in the book, your study of the book, Bible course notes, or chapter 10. An example is on page 36. (Note that the books are in canonical order, not alphabetical order.)

Special Problems

Synoptic Gospels

One problem in the filing of biblical materials is the similar content of the synoptic Gospels. While the literary function of a particular unit will differ in Matthew's Gospel from Mark's,

Chart 7

Organi-zational level	Broadest category (Level one)	Broad category (Level two)	Narrow category (Level three)	Narrowest category (Level four)
Outline indicator	I (Roman numerals)	A (Upper case letters)	1 (Arabic numerals)	a (Lower case letters)
Filing indicator	File drawer	Left cut/tab	Middle cut/tab	Right cut/tab
	Bible	*Genesis*	*1–2* *3* *4–5* *6–9* *and so forth*	*No narrowest categories means that I either never preached Genesis or did so with large units*
		Exodus	*No narrow categories means that I never studied Exodus beyond a survey of the book*	
		Leviticus	*1–7* *8–10* *11–16* *17–22* *23–27*	
		and so forth		

background research and certain observations will carry over and therefore should be accessible irrespective of which Gospel is being studied. There are several solutions to this problem. All solutions hinge on developing a chart that cross-references all similar or parallel passages.

Solution #1: Use a published synthetic outline and numbered folders

There are several published synthetic outlines of the Gospels that can be used to save the work of constructing your own synthetic outline. Hendriksen's commentary on Matthew[1] has such a listing. Other popular synthetic works on the Gospels are J. D. Pentecost's *The Words and Works of Jesus*

1. William Hendriksen, *Exposition of the Gospel According to Matthew*, New Testament Commentary Series (Grand Rapids: Baker Book House, 1973), 3–32.

Christ[2] and A. T. Robertson's *Harmony of the Gospels for Students of the Life of Christ*.[3] Chapter 10 is an adaptation of Robertson's work. This same approach could be used for the material in 1 and 2 Chronicles which parallels and overlaps much of the material in 1 and 2 Samuel and 1 and 2 Kings.[4]

Once a synthetic outline of the Gospels has been developed or otherwise secured, number each set of parallel passages and each unique passage on the cross-reference sheets, one number per set of parallel passages or unique passage. File your materials in the numbered folder which corresponds to the number for that passage.

An alternative solution is to pick one Gospel as the "core" (usually Mark) and to file any material under Mark if Mark includes it. Matthew is used if the material is not in Mark. Luke is used if the material is not in either Mark and Matthew. Finally, John is used for material unique to John. The cross-reference listing sheet tells you at a glance where to go to find the material for any passage.

Solution #2: Use one gospel and cross-reference sheets

A third solution is to ignore trying to correlate all of the parallel and related accounts and to file the material under the Gospel you studied when you found it. However, you still have to decide which Gospel will take precedence when filing material unrelated to a specific passage such as an article on a particular city Jesus ministered in, miracles, or parables. A synthetic outline (Solution #1) will be helpful for this.

Solution #3: File under the passage studied with cross-referencing

An additional question arises when filing Bible materials, "Where are survey-type materials filed?" The simplest answer is to make up a left tab folder with the title "OT Survey" and place it in your file just before Genesis. The same can be done for the New Testament, or a survey of several books such as the minor prophets, the Gospels, and so forth. Thematic surveys on topics such as eschatology, ecclesiology, anger, and so forth, should be filed in the appropriate folder in the theology or topical files section of your system.

Bible Survey Materials

A final addition that many people incorporate into their Bible section is a left tab folder with the title "OT Word Studies" placed before Genesis or after Malachi and a left tab folder with the title "NT Word Studies" placed before Matthew or after Revelation. Middle tab folders are used to hold the results of major word studies using one folder for each word study. Although it may seem inconsistent to put material in

Word Studies

2. Dwight Pentecost, *The Words and Works of Jesus Christ* (Grand Rapids: Zondervan Publishing House, 1981), 11–22.

3. Robertson, *Harmony of the Gospels for Students of the Life of Christ* (New York: Harper and Brothers, 1922).

4. William Day Crockett, *A Harmony of the Books of Samuel, Kings, and Chronicles* (Grand Rapids: Baker Book House, 1951).

the Bible section that is not technically tied to one passage, this strategy is easy to remember and keeps all of your word studies in a single place which is physically close to your Bible files.

It is best to do word studies on separate sheets of paper from the rest of a Bible study on a particular passage so that they can be filed separately. By simply writing a note on the top of the Bible study, referring to the word study done as a part of your study of the passage, the word study can always be reviewed when the passage is studied again.

Summary

In summary, the simple device of using a file drawer as a level of outline or organization makes for a very effective subordination system for Bible passages and keeps all Bible files together. Note that without the broadest category of "Bible," if each book of the Bible was a left tab, the books of the Bible files would not be filed in canonical or Bible order, since most systems file materials in alphabetical order. In addition, if "Bible" was a left tab, there would be insufficient subordination for teaching or preaching units. Thus, the device of making "Bible" into a broadest category corresponding to a file drawer provides the levels of subordination needed, keeps all Bible material together for easier access, and keeps Bible materials in canonical order. Special consideration needs to be given in some manner to parallel passages, survey material that spans more than one book of the Bible, and word studies.

Filing and Indexing Sermons and Bible Studies

5

Overview

This chapter will answer the following questions:

- Where can sermons, messages, and Bible studies be filed? What works best?
- Why does the exegetical work for a message need to be indexed? What is an easy way to do it?

Filing Sermons, Messages, and Bible Studies

Filing Possibilities

Every teacher or preacher must decide where to file materials developed for sermons, messages, and Bible studies.[1] Should they be filed:

under the title
under the topic
under the primary Bible passage used
under each Bible passage used
under a special section such as "Messages"
in the chronological sequence in which they were preached or taught
or on some other basis?

Perhaps the easiest way of filing these materials is to adopt the following procedure.

Sermons, messages, and studies based on a biblical text should be filed in the "Books of the Bible" file under the primary text the message was based on. The system discussed below is especially well suited for this purpose.[2]

Filing messages based on a biblical text

---

1. Those involved in nonvocational Christian work will not have as much of this material to file as a senior pastor will. Nevertheless, much will accumulate over a lifetime of ministry.
2. See chapter 10 for how these files can be organized.

Filing topical messages

Topical sermons, messages, and studies may be filed in one place or under the topic itself. Normally, filing all messages in one place is preferable because of the purpose for filing: to minimize the time spent finding so as to maximize the time for ministry.

Just as all illustrations, no matter what the topic, are kept together in one file because that is the easiest way to use them, so messages which are filed together are easier to use. Since messages are often used again (why else file them?), the easiest way to find them is to file them in one section.

In contrast, if sermons, messages, and Bible studies are filed under their appropriate topic and thus throughout a file system, the first step in finding a message would need to be consulting a master index. If several messages are to be reviewed before deciding which will be best for a particular situation, then several file drawers must be opened up to find the several messages and then all of the messages, except one, must be refiled in the several drawers. How much easier to have them in one section.

If messages are to be filed together, a left tab folder should be made with the title "Messages, Topical." Messages on subjects such as Abortion, Easter, Mother's Day, and so forth are filed in middle tab folders. Individual messages in a topical series are filed in right tab folders under a middle tab that identifies the series. In such a case, the middle tab folder is empty and serves only as a place marker. For example:

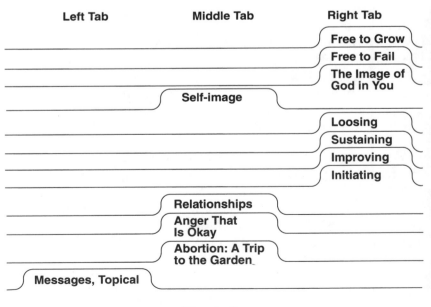

Left Tab	Middle Tab	Right Tab
		Free to Grow
		Free to Fail
		The Image of God in You
	Self-image	
		Loosing
		Sustaining
		Improving
		Initiating
	Relationships	
	Anger That Is Okay	
	Abortion: A Trip to the Garden	
Messages, Topical		

Chart 8

In summary, there is a way to file sermons, messages, and Bible studies which is simple, consistent, and flexible. Those based on a biblical text should be filed under that text. Those which are topical should be filed together under a left tab folder labeled "Messages, Topical." Then, the middle tab is labeled with the series title or the message title (if the message was not part of a series) and the right tab is labeled with the message titles for those messages that were part of a series.

Indexing Sermons, Messages, and Bible Studies

Special Concerns

More difficult than determining where to file materials developed for sermons, messages, and Bible studies is trying to retrieve research on a passage that was not filed under that passage. This may occur in two situations.

First, for many messages significant exegesis is done on passages other than the main text. Since the message cannot be filed under all of the passages studied (unless you love to make photocopies), where do you file the message? Some type of cross-referencing or indexing is the only solution.

For example, suppose that you preached a sermon from Romans 8 that deals with the ministry of the Holy Spirit in the life of the believer. In the sermon you spent ten minutes developing the concept of being filled with the Spirit (Eph. 5:18) and relating it to the leading of the Spirit in Romans 8. You probably did a lot of careful exegetical and homiletical work on Ephesians 5:18 that you need to be able to retrieve in a few years when you preach on Ephesians. Of course, right now you know where the Ephesians 5:18 material is, but in a few years when several hundred other sermons have come between you and Romans 8 you may find yourself thinking: "I know I did some work on this before, but where is it?" To repeat all of your exegetical and homiletical work because you can't find your old work is wasteful. Thus, some kind of indexing or cross-referencing is essential.

The second situation that calls for indexing is topical work. Topical sermons, messages, and studies typically cover several major passages at a level that would be beneficial to retrieve in the future. Somehow, all of the research done on those passages needs to be indexed so that it can be found in the future when needed. In addition, since topical messages frequently have clever titles that bear only a degree of relationship to the actual topic of the message, it is important that the topic itself be indexed.

The McComb Bible Indexing System

Step 1: Obtain a Bible for indexing

Step 2: Decide how you will file your messages

Step 3: Write in the location of the message in the index Bible

The McComb Bible indexing system addresses these problems in a simple, comprehensive, and flexible manner. It is capable of meeting almost any set of indexing needs.[3]

Obtain a Bible with a concordance that you will designate as your index book. The translation used is irrelevant as the Bible will be used for indexing only, not reading. Wide-margin Bibles are ideal.

Decide how you will file your messages, sermons, and Bible studies. Dr. McComb numbered every sermon in the order preached (that is, 1, 2, 3, 4, 5. . . .) and filed them in numerical order, ten messages to a folder. Others prefer to file their textual sermons in their Bible file under the passage itself and their topical sermons in a folder under "Messages, Topical."

When you are ready to file a sermon, message, or Bible study, open your index Bible to the passage(s) used and write in the margin of the Bible the location of the sermon (that is, the title of the folder it is in). Obviously it is essential to index only those passages for which a significant amount of research was done. It is the exegetical research that will prove valuable in the future.

If a biblical paragraph was the basis for the message, then you should note it by bracketing the passage in the Bible or by writing in the margin "vs.17–33, #76" (or whatever the title of the folder is that has the message and its research).

For any message, textual or topical, for which you did research on more than one major text that you may want to use in the future, you can easily note the location of the material next to the main passage as well as next to the other significant texts studied.

Messages that are filed in a Bible file corresponding exactly to the verses bracketed in the index Bible should use an abbreviation system to indicate "the message on Mark 4:1–20 is filed in the Bible file as a right tab with the title 'Mark 4:1–20, What's Growing in Your Life?'" BF is an effective abbreviation for "Bible File." BF would mean that the message desired is filed in the Bible file for this passage. If the location is under a different passage, merely write that passage in the margin of the index Bible without noting BF because the Bible reference indicates that the message is in the Bible file. If the material is in a topical file, write in TF (you guessed it, TF means Topical File) and the exact title of the folder.

Messages that are filed on a computer can be indexed in exactly the same manner by using the notation CF for "Computer File" and then a reference to the appropriate file or disk.

3. This indexing system was developed by a now-deceased Presbyterian pastor, Dr. John Hess McComb. He showed it to the author and it has since benefited many pastors and Bible teachers.

If you taught a Bible study on self-image you would file it and index the major passages as described above. The difficulty occurs when a few years after giving the message, you remember doing a study on self-image, but do not remember what passages you used or its title. Without either of these pieces of information, how can you find the message?

If your index Bible has a concordance and it is used as an index of *topics* (not titles) the problem is solved. You simply write in "self-image" (the term "self-image" does not occur in the Bible) in the "S" section of the concordance and next to it the file location of the message.

The advantage of a wide-margin Bible is that it provides more room for your notations. If your topic term is already in the concordance, so much the easier. In addition, you can index a study under several topics if they seem appropriate to you. This is a necessity when doing topical messages and helpful with textual messages that deal with a major topic.

The blank pages at the back of your McComb Index Bible can be used to keep a list of textual and topical series and special purpose messages (evangelistic, youth, funeral, retreat series, and so forth).

Summary

The value of the McComb Index Bible approach is that in one book you have an index to any study of specific Scripture passages you have ever done. The book fits neatly on a bookshelf, needs no special file box as cards do, can never be misfiled as can happen with cards, cannot lose a page as can happen with cards, and is economical, permanent, and durable.

Filing Illustrations

6

This chapter will answer the following question:

- What are some guidelines or principles to help the beginner in filing illustrative material?

Principles for Filing Illustrations

Many speakers record illustrations on 3x5 or 4x6 cards. The following discussion assumes that this method will be used. However, the principles will apply to any method of storing illustrations. Computer data bases offer the added potential for extensive cross-referencing and quick retrieval.[1]

Recording Illustrations

File under broad headings since most illustrations fit several specific applications or can easily be modified to do so. This rule for filing will keep your material available at the broadest appropriate level. In addition, the use of broad headings lends consistency and logic to the file and helps the user to avoid the kind of highly personalized heading that sounds good at the moment but ultimately becomes nonretrievable. The first word of a heading should be a noun rather than a modifying word such as an adverb or adjective.

File under Broad Headings

For example, an illustration of a beautiful sunset should not be filed under "Beautiful Sunset" but under either "Sunset" or probably better yet, under "Creation, Beauty of."

An illustration of choosing happiness in the midst of a severe

---

1. To be fast enough for usefulness, a hard drive and a relatively fast computer should be used. Some older machines are decidedly slower than filing and retrieving illustrations from a card file box. A number of data bases can be used for filing illustrations. The basic requirements are ability to hold several thousand illustrations, ability to do extensive cross-referencing, ability to keep Bible books in canonical order rather than alphabetical order, ability to revise existing illustrations (including a note for when and where used) and the ability to add new illustrations. An excellent system that does all of this and comes with a base of over 1600 illustrations is *Illustrations for Biblical Preaching-Mac for the Apple Macintosh*. It is available from Illustrations for Biblical Preaching-Mac, P.O. Box 06746, Ft. Myers, FL 33906. An MS-Dos (IBM compatible) version is available from The Pastor's Autoillustrator, P.O. Box 5056, Greeley, CO 80631.

trial should not be filed under "Choosing Happiness" but under either "Happiness" or under "Choices" or "Decisions." In this case a good topic might be "Choices, for Happiness" with a cross-reference under the heading "Trials" where you would see the notation "See: Choices, for Happiness."

Use Subheadings When Needed

Most illustrations are specific enough to need a subheading which further describes the illustration. In categories with only a few cards, this step isn't as helpful as in those categories such as "Evangelism," "Children," and "Church" which tend to become quite large. In addition, the use of standard subheadings is helpful. To some degree these standardizations are arbitrary but, once you get used to them, you will find that they save time. No subheading should be used when the illustration is of a general nature.

Some commonly used subheading terms follow.[2]

Application of	Necessity of
Benefit of	Purpose for
Example of	Requirements for
Definition/Description of	Results/Consequences of
Humorous	Response to
Lack of	Source of
Motive for	Value of

Use Cross-Referencing

Many illustrations can be used to illustrate not only different aspects of one topic but different topics. In addition, many illustrations directly refer to other topics. In these cases cross-referencing will enable you to retrieve the illustration when needed.

When the cross-reference is not unique to the illustration at hand but instead reflects some kind of logical relationship between the two topics, then the cross-referencing should be done with a general topic-to-topic cross-reference and a separate cross-reference card for both topics. Note that cross-referencing can be to a general topic or to a specific subtopic.

When the cross-reference is unique to the illustration at hand then put the cross-reference on the card with the illustration and make up a cross-reference card to file under the other topic.

Cross-referencing of the topic-to-topic kind should be noted in the index of topics list you use. Some examples of topic-to-topic cross-referencing follow.

Illustrations for "Obedience" often can be found under "Childrearing" and "Discipline" and should be so cross-referenced by using a topic-to-topic cross-reference card.

---

2. Michael P. Green, *Illustrations for Biblical Preaching* (Grand Rapids: Baker Book House, 1989).

Illustrations for "Trials" can often be found under topics such as "Discipline, Purpose of," "Pain, Reason for," "Suffering," and "Testing." Again, these several topic-to-topic cross-references need not be noted on each card filed under "Trials" but can all be put on one cross-reference card.

A specific illustration on the temporary nature of wealth probably would be filed under "Wealth, Temporary Nature of." However, if the illustration relied on the inevitability of death then a cross-reference to "Death" would be useful and should be made on the illustration card as a reverse reference as well as on a cross-reference card under "Death."

File under Topics, not Bible Passages

The vast majority of illustrations should be filed under a topic, not a particular passage. The reason for this rule is that you will preach a topic many times to a group, but will probably preach a specific passage only once. Thus filing illustrations under specific passages makes them inaccessible unless you happen to look under that passage. There are two exceptions to this rule.

The first exception occurs when an illustration is so specific that it is only useful with one verse in the entire Bible.

The second exception occurs in the form of a cross-reference from the passage or verse to the topic under which the illustration was filed. This should occur only when that topic would not come to mind when preparing a message on that verse.

For example, there is no need to cross-reference Romans 3:23 to an illustration filed under "Sin." Anyone who wouldn't look up "Sin" while preaching on that verse should not be preaching! However, if there was a great illustration of "falling short" under "Self-Image" then a cross-reference card should be made up. Of course, if an index book is used, many such cross-references should be entered in it.

Avoid Undocumented, Out-of-Date, and Misinterpreted Quotes and Statistics

There is an old saying that statistics don't lie, but statisticians do. Unless you are absolutely sure of the reliability and correct interpretation of a statistic, you are wise to not use it. Most preachers are not trained in statistical analysis. As a result some have been guilty of making horrifying statements that are simply not true and which are recognized as such by those in the audience who are trained in numerical analysis. *A wrong or unwise use of statistics will put a shadow of doubt over the reliability of the rest of the message.* In a society that is undergoing rapid social change, statistical descriptions of that society are often out of date by the time they get published. In addition, predictions based on current trends are almost guaranteed to be wrong.[3]

3. The reason for this is very simple, most "predictions" are based on a linear or straight-line projection of the present trend and yet most trends are anything but linear.

Additional concerns

Many statistics are useful for illustrations. For example, consider these three types:

Historical or descriptive statistics should be properly referenced and from a reliable source.

Timeless statistics such as the size of the universe as a reflection of the majesty of God, are often useful.

Predictive statistics that are properly researched may be useful. For example, census projections prepared by the federal government.

Pithy one-liners should be used with care. Often their impact is determined by the personality and speaking style of the user. In other words, just because it worked for someone else doesn't mean that it will work for you.

Quotations from written sources should be used with equal care. There is a difference between the impact a statement has when in print and how it sounds orally. There is a difference between reading and listening. In addition the passages that impact you as a reader often do so because of all that you read before. In oral communication you will not read the full context of a quotation and thus the insight and force of the quotation is often lost on the hearers.

Personalization is an element of preaching style and of communication. Consider the psalms. Although clearly arising out of personal experiences, the psalmist generally obscures that experience. The result is that these "depersonalized" psalms become highly "personalized" for the hearer. The same is true of illustrations. At times a personalized illustration can be very effective. However, at other times the removal of personalized elements can render the illustration more effective.

Summary of Principles for Filing Illustrations

In summary, the following principles should guide your filing of illustrations.

1. File under broad headings, not specific ones.
2. Use subheadings when needed.
3. Use cross-referencing when needed.
4. File under topics, not Bible passages, except for illustrations useful for only a particular passage.
5. Use cross-referencing for topical illustrations fitting for a passage unrelated to the topic.
6. Avoid undocumented, out-of-date, and misinterpreted quotes and statistics.

Beginning a Filing System

7

Overview

This chapter will answer the following questions:

•What are some helpful ideas and suggestions for those just beginning to construct a filing system?
•How can a computer be used to make filing easier?

General Suggestions

Beginning Steps

When beginning a filing system, purchase three or four boxes of folders. Then you will have more than enough folders and won't be tempted to omit a folder because you are running out of them or out of that particular cut.

File cabinets

Budget for a good quality four drawer file cabinet. Look for one with "full suspension drawers." Avoid the budget cabinets. Their drawers don't pull out fully and the glides tend to work hard or stick. The money saved is not even close to the years of annoyance that these cabinets offer. If space is limited, two two-drawer file cabinets can be used as pedestals for a desk made out of a door or other large solid surface.

Labels

If you use labels on your folders, when making additional folders after you have your system up and functioning, you have two options.

Type out a label immediately.

Make up the folder with the title penciled in on the tab. Every few weeks/months roll the typewriter over to your files, open the drawers, type out the labels you need, and put them on the folders already in the drawers.

Color coding

Some people like to color code their files. In the topic-subtopic system, each separate broadest area (or file drawer level of organization) can have its own label color. In this way refiling is made easier as it is faster to go to the blue drawer than to think through which broadest category the folder goes in. Of course the color of the files within a drawer should be noted on the outside of the drawer. Color coding of different tabs within a broadest category is redundant.

Articles

When you see something that you want to keep and therefore file, write in the top right hand corner of the item the location in your file where it will go. If you are reading a personal copy of a magazine, note this file location when you decide to keep the article and tear it out for filing later.

Those using the separately indexed approach should simply write on the item the filing topic to be used if it can be remembered. If not, a brief descriptive term should be written to save the time of rereading the article. By writing the filing location on the top of the article, anyone can file or refile the article without asking you to decide or remember under which heading it should be filed.

Consider the following examples where the actual file the material will be placed in is in **bold**. These examples are in the format: Left Cut—Middle Cut—Right Cut for a topic-subtopic filing system. A separately indexed approach would merely list the one word or phrase that appears in bold.

The "To Be Filed" box

If you dislike filing new material or refiling folders, put an open box (the one the folders came in) on top of your file cabinet. Put your "To Be Filed" materials in this box. Then every week at an appointed time (such as Friday afternoon) file or refile everything in the box.

Another idea

First (left) and third (right) cut folders are interchangeable by simply turning one inside out.

Husband and wife systems

Spouses should be very careful about integrating their file systems, especially if both intend to be involved in ministry. An integrated system requires that the files be kept at a mutually accessible location, usually home. The difficulty is that this location is usually not where most of your ministry work is done. As a result, couples with a single filing system are constantly carrying files to work and back home. In addition, one spouse may wish to file items that the other wouldn't, file material in different places, mark up an article that the other wanted unmarked, and so forth. This can create chaos.

Class and seminar notes

It is often best to keep class notes, lecture series, seminar notes, and similar materials that come out of a context where you were personally involved in a notebook or folder for two or three years. Then break them up and file them where they best fit. This is for two reasons.

First, in situations where you have personal involvement, you often will remember initially by associating the material with the teacher, and only later by thinking of the actual topic. For example, you probably will recall a clear exposition of a passage by remembering the professor who gave it, not the class it was a part of. Thus, it is best to keep these materials in a form that corresponds to how you will remember them. However, after two or three years, professors and courses begin to fade and blend together. At this point, break up the notebook and file the materials where they belong. In a theology course this will be quite simple. In a Christian education course this might be more complex as part of the course might fit under "Leadership," part under "Sunday School—Job Descriptions," part under "Counseling," and so forth.

The second reason for this strategy is that time gives perspective. Often students are so enthusiastic about a topic after taking a course or attending a seminar that they will put together twenty or more folders to cover the area. However, after three or more years they find that they don't use the material that much and two or three folders probably would do. But now it is too late as there are a large number of folders to lug around and a lot of time was devoted to developing something no one is using. This violates the goal of filing of "minimize time spent filing and finding materials so as to maximize time for ministry."

Computers

Computers have the potential to be helpful for setting up and maintaining a filing system. However, they can add complication and confusion. Thus it is wise to consider what a computer can and cannot do and your own personal abilities and preferences before deciding to "computerize" your filing system.

Word Processing

Computers use programs to accomplish specific tasks. These programs are called software and come on disks that are inserted into a computer. By far the most popular type of computer program is the word-processing program. These programs work with words. Think of them as extremely sophisticated typewriters.

A computer can use a word-processing program to develop and modify a listing of all of the file headings or topics in a filing system. Users of either separately indexed systems or topic-subtopic systems probably will find a word processor a great time-saver in the construction of their filing system.

Value to separately indexed filing systems

Word processors are especially useful for those using a separately indexed type of filing system. Instead of developing an index book that must last a lifetime or be retyped if it wears out, the word processor can simply print out a new index book.

Of particular help to those using a separately indexed system is that it is very easy to add cross-references to an index if the word processor has a Sort command. Simply type in the cross-reference(s) under the topic. When done, the Sort command will relocate the cross-references to their proper place in the index. If your word processor does not have this feature, simply move to that part of the alphabet where the cross-reference belongs and type in the cross-reference and the phrase "See: (name of the topic)."

Data Base

Another form of software that computers use is the data base. Data base programs work with data such as addresses, purchase orders, and so forth. Some data base programs are easy to use for filing. A data base or hypertext program can enable you to develop an extensive system of cross-referencing as you build your system without having to move to the part of the alphabet where the cross-reference term occurs. These cross-references can be printed out as a part of your index book. Selecting the right data base and allowing yourself time to learn how to use the software can result in significant time savings.

Potential Difficulties

The difficulties that come with using a computer are all potential. They do not have to occur and can be avoided with forethought.

The first potential difficulty occurs when the index to a filing system is kept only on the computer. If it is necessary to turn on a computer, load a different program, or open a separate computer file just to find one file folder, then such an approach to filing is not simple. In addition, such a system probably would not be easy to use for a part-time office helper or a temporary secretary. The solution is to remember that all separately indexed systems need a printed index book.

The second potential problem can result from software and hardware changes. Software is often built around the particular abilities of a machine and will not always work on a different or a newer machine. In addition software programs are constantly being updated and abandoned. What will you do if the software you use for your indexing is abandoned by its maker (or the maker goes out of business)? How will you move your data to another program when need to arises in the future? For those who have a widely used machine such as an IBM compatible or an Apple Macintosh, these problems are usually resolved by the software developers. However, for those whose machine uses unique software or is built on different hardware, this is a potential problem. Normally, if all you have used is a word processor, you can format your file into an ASCII text file which is usually readable by other computers.

If you have used a data base, it is wise to be sure that the data format your program uses can be transferred to other machines and programs.

Conclusion

Remember that any filing system should help you to be a better steward of that which God has entrusted to you. A filing system has no purpose of its own. There is no inherent moral goodness in neat files, they are simply a tool to be used to help you be faithful.

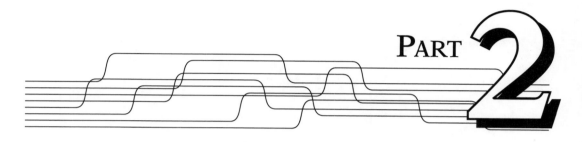

PART 2

Sample Filing Systems

A Sample of a Separately Indexed Filing System

8

The following listing is a sample of a separately indexed filing system. All of the files in this system are organized in a topic-subtopic system in chapter 9. The word *See* is a reference to related files. The word *Use* is a reference to the file where the desired material is located.

A

Abortion
See:
Crisis Pregnancy Center
Pregnancy, Unwanted
Pregnancy, Unmarried

Adam
Use: Eden, Prefall State

Administration

Adolescence
See:
Youth

Adoption

Adult Choirs

Adult Department Curriculum

Adultery

Advent

Advertising
Use: Publicity

Agnosticism
See:
Heresies

AIDS

Alcoholism
See:
Substance Abuse

American Bible Society

Amillennialism
See:
Millennium

Ancestor Worship

Angels, Bad
Use: Demons

Angels, Good

Anger

Animism

Annual Meeting

Annual Report, 1992

Annual Report, 1993

Anthropological Argument
   for God
See:
   Theistic Arguments

Anthropology
See:
   Eden, Prefall State
   Harmatology
   Image of God
   Original Sin
   Seven Deadly Sins
   Soul

Antichrist

Anxiety
See:
   Worry

Apologetics
See:
   Anthropological
      Argument
   Cosmological Argument
   Ontological Argument
   Teleological Argument
   Theistic Arguments

Apostasy
See:
   Heresies

Apostolic Age
   Use: Church History,
      Early

Archeology

Art

Artificial Insemination
   See:
   Childbearing
   Sterility

Ascension
   Use: Christ, Ascension

Assurance, of Salvation

Astrology

Atheism

Atonement
   See:
   Limited/Unlimited
      Atonement

Attributes of God
   See:
   Specific name of
      attribute

Audio Visual
   See:
   Catalogs
   Films
   Overhead Projector
      Masters
   Slide Library Index
   Tape Library Index
   Tapes

Auto Title

AWANA

Awards Catalogs

B

Baby Dedication, Ceremony

Baby Dedication,
   Certificates

Baby Dedication, Records

Babylon

Bahai

Bank Statements

Baptism
   See:
   Ordinances

Baptism, Certificates

Baptism, Committee Job
   Description

Baptism, Handout for
   Prospect

Baptism, Modes

Baptism, of Holy Spirit
   See:
   Pneumatology

Baptism, Policies &
   Procedures

Baptism, Records

Baptist

Benedictions

Benevolence, Committee
   Records

Benevolence, Policies, &
   Procedures

Betting
   Use: Gambling

Bible Study Fellowship

Bible, Conferences

Bible, Discussion Notes

Bible, Geography

Bible, Reading Schedules

Bible, Studies

Biblical Theology
   See:
   Old Testament Theology

New Testament Theology
Johannine Theology
Pauline Theology
Petrine Theology

Bibliology
   See:
   Canonicity & Authority
   Covenant Theology
   Dispensational Theology
   Illumination
   Inerrancy
   Inspiration
   Interpretation
      (Hermeneutics)
   Revelation, General
   Revelation, Special

Birth Control

Blended Family

Blood Drive

Board Game Night
   See:
   Recreation

Book Reviews

Books to Purchase List

Brethren Assemblies

Brochures

Buddhism

Budget

Budgeting

Building Plans
   See:
   Facilities
   Maintenance Agreements
   Rental Agreements and
      Policies

Bulletin Board Ideas

Bulletin File, 1992

Bulletin File, 1993

Bulletin Insert Ideas

Burnout

C

Camp Alwaysrains

Camp Lotsabugs

Camp, Family

Camp, Programs, Adult

Camp, Programs, General

Camp, Programs, Youth

Camp, Promotional Ideas

Camp, Recreation Ideas

Camp, Summer Youth

Camp, Worship Ideas

Campus Crusade

Canonicity & Authority

Capital Punishment
See:
Crime & Punishment

Catalogs

Catholic, Roman
Use: Roman Catholic

CBMC

Celibacy
See:
Abstinence

Charismatics
See:
Pentecostals

Child Abuse

Childbearing
See:
Abortion
Adoption
Artificial Insemination
Birth Control
Infertility
Pregnancy, Unmarried

Pregnancy, Unwanted/
Unplanned
Sterility

Child Care

Child Evangelism
Fellowship

Children's Choirs

Children's Church

Children, Nature & Needs

Children, Spiritual Training
of

Choir Committee

Choir Equipment

Choir Instruments

Choir Music

Choir Robes

Christ, Ascension

Christ, Baptism

Christ, Birth

Christ, Death

Christ, Deity

Christ, Offices

Christ, Incarnation

Christ, Resurrection
Use: Resurrection

Christ, Second Coming
Use: Rapture

Christ, Transfiguration
Use: Transfiguration

Christ, Virgin Birth
Use: Virgin Birth

Christian & Missionary
Alliance

Christian Education
See:
Sunday School
Vacation Bible School

Christian Education Board

Christian Science

Christmas

Church
See: Ecclesiology

Church, Brochure

Church, Constitution

Church, Correspondence, 1992

Church, Correspondence, 1993

Church, Discipline

Church, Offices
    See:
    Deacons
    Elders
    Trustees

Church, Organizational Chart

Church, Picnic

Church, Universal (Organism)

Churches Alive

Church History, American

Church History, Early

Church History, Medieval

Church History, Reformation

College Department

College Records

Colleges

Communion
    Use: Lord's Supper

Computer

Confucianism

Correspondence, Personal, 1992

Correspondence, Personal, 1993

Cosmological Argument for God

Counseling, Bibliography

Counseling, Conferences

Counseling, Correspondence, 1992

Counseling, Correspondence, 1993

Counseling, Premarital
    See:
    Engagement, Studies

Counseling, Seminar Notes, 6/91

Covenant Theology

Creationism/Evolution

Crime & Punishment
    See:
    Capital Punishment

Crisis Pregnancy Center

Cults
    Use: Specific group

D

Dating

Deacons
    See:
    Church, Offices

Deacons, Potential

Death, Acceptance of Another's

Death, Acceptance of Own

Death Penalty
    Use: Capital Punishment

Debate

Decision Making & the Will of God

Decrees of God

Demons
   Use: Satan & Demons

Demonstration

Depression

Devotional Life

Devotionals

Directory

Discipleship

Discipline (Family)
   Use:
   Church, Discipline

Discussion

Dispensational Theology

Divorce

Doctrinal Statement

Doubtful Things

Dramatization

Dreams

Drinking
   Use: Alcoholism

Drugs
   See:
   Substance Abuse Issues

E

Easter

Ecclesiology
   See:
   Baptism
   Church (various
      headings)
   Foot Washing
   Lord's Supper
   Polity

Eden, Prefall State

Education
   See:
   Christian Education
   Colleges
   Sex Education
   Seminaries

Elders
   See:
   Church, Officers
   Elders, Potential

Election
   See:
   Predestination

Elementary School
      Literature

Emergency & Disaster
   Plans

Engagement Studies,
   Adjusting

Engagement Studies,
   Adjusting Financially

Engagement Studies,
   Adjusting Physically

Engagement Studies,
   Adjusting Spiritually

Engagement Studies,
   Ceremony Ideas
   (poems, songs, and so
   forth)

Engagement Studies,
   Honeymoon

Engagement Studies, Legal
   Issues

Engagement Studies,
   Parenthood

Engagement Studies,
   Sexual Issues

Epiphany

Equipment Manuals

Eschatology
   See:
   Amillennialism
   Antichrist
   Eternal State
   Heaven
   Hell

Judgment
Messianic Prophecy
Millennium
Premillennialism
Rapture

Eternal State
See:
Heaven
Hell

Eternity

Ethics
See: Specific Issue

Eucharist
Use: Lord's Supper

Euthanasia

Evangelical Free

Evangelical Movement

Evangelism

Evangelism Bibliography

Evangelism Committee
Notes

Evangelism Explosion

Evangelism Literature
See:
Trustee

Evil

Evolution
Use: Creation/Evolution

F

Facilities

Faith

Fall
See:
Harmatology
Sin, Original

Family
See:
Children
Discipline
Home
Parents

Family Camp

Family Night Ideas

Fasting

Father's Day

Fear

Feminism
See:
Women, Role in Church
Women, Role in Family

Fighting, Rules for

Filling, of Spirit

Films

Finances
See:
Budget
Money
Stewardship

Floor Plans, Church

Follow Up of New Believers
See:
Discipleship

Foot Washing
See:
Ordinances

Forum

Freedom

Friendship

Fruit of Spirit
See:
Pneumatology

Fundamentalist

Funerals, Ceremony

Funerals, Cremation

Funerals, Music Selections

Funerals, Records of

Funerals, Scriptures for

G

Gambling
Use: Betting

Games
Use: Youth Ministry,
Activities

Gifts of Spirit
See:
Pneumatology

Giving
Use: Stewardship

Giving Records

Glorification

Goals, Current Family

Goals, Current Personal

God
See:
Attributes of God
Decrees of God
Eternity
Freedom
Goodness
Holiness
Immutability

Justice
Love
Mercy
Names of God
Omnipotence
Omnipresence
Omniscience
Predestination
Sovereignty
Theism
Theology Proper
Trinitarianism
Truthfulness
Wisdom

Good Friday

Good News Clubs

Goodness

Gospel

Gospel Presentations

Gossip

Grace

Graduation

Greed

Greek Grammar Notes

Greek Verb Charts

Greek Vocabulary Lists

Groups
Use: Small Groups

Guilt

H

Handicapped Child

Harmatology
See:
Fall
Sin, Original

Health Needs

Health Records

Heaven
See:
Eternal State
Eternity

Hebrew Grammar Notes

Hebrew Verb Charts

Hebrew Vocabulary Lists

Hell
See:
Eternal State
Eternity

Heresies (Antitheistic)

Hermeneutics
Use: Interpretation

High School Literature

Hinduism

Historical Theology
See: Church History

Holiness

Holy Spirit
See:
Baptism, Holy Spirit
Filling, Holy Spirit
Fruit of Spirit
Gifts of Spirit
Indwelling of Spirit
Pneumatology
Sealing of Spirit
Types & Symbols of the
Holy Spirit

Home, Bibliography

Homiletics

Homosexuality

Humanism

Hymns
Use: Music, Church

I

Idolatry

Illumination

Image of God

Immutability

Incarnation
See: Virgin Birth

Incest

Indwelling, of Holy Spirit
See:
Pneumatology

Inerrancy, of Bible
See:
Bibliology
Canonicity & Authority

Infants (0-2)

Infant Dedication
Use: Baby Dedication

Inferiority

Infertility
See:
Artificial Insemination
Childbearing
Sterility

Inner-City Mission

Inspiration, of Bible
See:
Bibliology

Insurance

Interpretation
(Hermeneutics)
See:
Bibliology

InterVarsity

Inventory

"Inviting Your Neighbor"
handouts

Islam

Israel
See:
Jews
Judaism

J

Jail Ministry

Jehovah's Witness

Jesus Christ
Use: Christ

Jews
See:
Israel
Judaism

Job Descriptions

Johannine Theology

Judaism
See:
Israel
Jews

Judgment

Junior Choirs

Junior Church

Junior High Department

Justice

Justification

K

Kids vs Parents Quiz Show

Kindergarten (4-5)

L

Latin

Latin Grammar Notes

Latin Verb Charts

Latin Vocabulary Lists

Latter Day Saints
Use Mormonism

Leadership

Lecture

Lent

Liberation Theology

Limited/Unlimited
Atonement
See:
Atonement

Loneliness

Lord's Prayer

Lord's Supper

Lord's Supper, Ceremony

Lord's Supper, Committee
Job Description

Lord's Supper, Policies &
Procedures

Lord's Supper, Scripture
Readings

Lordship Salvation

Love

Lutheran

Lying

M

Maintenance Agreements

Manuals & Warranties

Marriage
See:
Counseling
Engagement Studies

Marriage, Bibliography

Marriage, Ceremonies

Marriage, Conferences

Marriage, Music

Marriage, Records

Marriage, Service Outlines

Martyrdom

Masturbation

Materialism

Meditation

Membership, Active

Membership, Application
Form

Membership, Discipline

Membership, Inactive

Membership, Lists

Membership, Mailings Only

Memorization

Mennonite

Mental Illness
  See:
  Counseling
  Specific topics

Mercy

Messianic Prophecy

Methodist

Millennium

Miracles

Mission Sunday

Missions

Missions, Annual
  Conference

Missions, Job Descriptions

Missions, Speakers

Missions, Support Policies

Missions, Supporting
  Agencies & Individuals

Money
  See: Stewardship

Mormonism

Mother's Day

Moving-Up Day

Music
  See:
  Choirs (listed by age
    grouping)

Music, Bibliography

Music, Church

N

Names of God

Navigators

Neighborhood Evangelistic
  Bible Studies

Neighborhood Strategy
  (Evangelism)

New Age Movement

New Testament Theology
  See:
  Biblical Theology

Newsletter, Current Issue

Newsletter, Ideas

Newsletters, 1992

Newsletters, 1993

Newspaper Ads

Nursery (2-3)

Nursery Department

O

Occult

Offerings
  See:
  Stewardship
  Tithe

Old Testament Theology
  See:
  Biblical Theology

Omnipotence

Omnipresence

Omniscience

Ontological Argument, for
    God
  See:
  Theistic Arguments

Order Records

Ordinances
  See:
  Baptism
  Footwashing
  Lord's Supper

Ordination, Ceremony

Ordination, Records
  Original Sin
  See:
  Fall
  Harmatology
  Sin

Overhead Projector Masters

P

Pain & Suffering

Panel (Teaching Method)

Parachurch Agencies
  See:
  Specific agencies

Parents Letters & Take
    Homes

Parents, Role of
  Pauline Theology
  See:
  Biblical Theology

Pentecost

Pentecostal
  See:
  Charismatics

Personality

Personnel Information

Peterine Theology
  See:
  Biblical Theology

Philosophy

Pneumatology
  See:
  Baptism, of Holy Spirit
  Filling, of Holy Spirit
  Fruit, of Holy Spirit
  Gifts, of Holy Spirit
  Indwelling, of Holy Spirit
  Sealing, of Holy Spirit
  Types & Symbols of the
    Holy Spirit

Policies

Policy Handbook

Polity

Polytheism

Poor

Pornography

Potential Workers

Praise

Prayer

Prayer Lists

Prayer Unanswered,
    Answers for

Preaching
  Use:
  Homiletics

Predestination
  See:
  Election

Pregnancy, Unmarried
  See:
  Abortion
  Crisis Pregnancy Center

Pregnancy,
    Unwanted/Unplanned
  See:
  Abortion
  Crisis Pregnancy Center

Premillennialism
  See:
  Millennialism

Presbyterian

Primary Church

Primary Department (6-8)

Problem Solving

Process of Teaching

Procrastination

Projects (Teaching Method)

Prolegomena
See:
Agnosticism
Creationism/Evolution
Heresies (Antitheistic)
Humanism
Liberation Theology
Materialism
Polytheism
Science

Publicity Committee
See:
Advertising
Brochures
Bulletin Board Ideas
Bulletin Insert Ideas
Church Brochure
"I Need Publicity" Forms
Newspaper Ads

Puppet Ministry

Q

Question and Answer
(Teaching method)

Quiet Time
Use: Devotional Life

R

Rapture

Rebellious Child

Redemption
See:
Soteriology

Reformation

Reincarnation
See:
Hinduism

Religions
See:
Ancestor Worship
Animism
Atheism
Bahai
Baptist
Brethren
Buddhism
Christian & Missionary
Alliance
Christian Science
Confucianism
Evangelical Free
Evangelical Movement
Fundamentalism
Hinduism
Islam

Jehovah's Witness
Judaism
Lutheran
Mennonite
Methodist
Mormonism
New Age Movement
Pentecostal
Presbyterian
Religions, Non-Christian
Roman Catholic
Seventh Day Adventist
Shintoism
Taoism
Unity

Rental Agreements and
Policies

Repentance

Resumé

Resurrection

Retirement

Retirement Home Ministry

Revelation, General
See:
Bibliology

Revelation, Special
See:
Bibliology

Robert's Rules of Order

Role Playing (Teaching
Method)

Roman Catholic

Roman Road
    See:
    Evangelism

S

Sabbath
    Use: Sunday

Salvation
    See:
    Assurance of Salvation
    Atonement
    Faith
    Glorification
    Gospel
    Grace
    Justification
    Limited/Unlimited
        Atonement
    Lordship Salvation
    Redemption
    Repentance
    Sanctification
    Soteriology

Sanctification

Satan & Demons

Schedule

Science

Sealing, of Holy Spirit
    See:
    Pneumatology

Secretary

Self-Discipline

Seminaries

Seminary Records

Senility
    See:
    Aging

Senior High Department

Senior Servants Ministry

Seven Deadly Sins
    See:
    Harmatology
    Sin

Seventh Day Adventist

Sex Education, Articles

Sex Education,
    Bibliography

Sex Education, Home
    Responsibilities

Shintoism

Sickness

Sin
    See:
    Fall
    Harmatology
    Original Sin

Single Adult Department

Single Parenting

Slide Library Index

Small Groups

Soteriology
    See:
    Assurance of Salvation
    Atonement
    Faith
    Glorification
    Gospel
    Grace
    Justification
    Limited/Unlimited
        Atonement
    Lordship Salvation
    Redemption
    Repentance
    Salvation
    Sanctification

Soul
    See:
    Anthropology

Soul Winning
    Use: Evangelism

Sovereignty of God

Spanish Grammar Notes

Spanish Verb Charts

Spanish Vocabulary Lists

Special Dates, January

Special Dates, February

Special Dates, March

Special Dates, April

Special Dates, May

Special Dates, June

Special Dates, July

Special Dates, August

Special Dates, September

Special Dates, October

Special Dates, November

Special Dates, December

Spiritual Life
  See:
  Discipleship
  Specific Issues

Spiritual Gifts
  Use: Gifts of the Spirit

Staff

Staff Retreat

Sterility
  See:
  Artificial Insemination
  Childbearing
  Infertility

Stewardship Campaign
  Ideas

Stewardship
  See:
  Money

Storytelling

Strategy for Anytown

Stress

Substance Abuse Issues
  See:
  Alcoholism
  Drugs

Suffering
  Use: Pain & Suffering

Suicide

Sunday Evening Service
  Worksheets

Sunday Morning Service
  Worksheets

Sunday School

Sunday School, Attendance
  Records

Sunday School,
  Convention, 1992

Sunday School, Teachers

Sunday Service Master
  Calendar: Themes &
  Messages

Super Bowl Sunday

Surveys

T

Taoism

Tabernacle

Tape Library Index

Tapes

Tax Records, Federal
  Income

Tax Records, Sales

Tax Records, State Income

Teaching Methods
  See:
  Debate
  Demonstration
  Discussion
  Dramatization
  Forum
  Lecture

Memorization
Panel
Problem Solving
Projects
Question & Answer
Role Playing
Storytelling
Topical research

Teacher Evaluations

Teacher Job Descriptions

Teacher Training Day

Teleological Argument, for
    God
    See:
    Theistic Arguments

Television

Temper
    Use: Anger

Tests

Thanksgiving

Theism

Theistic Arguments
    See:
    Anthropological
        Argument
    Cosmological Argument
    Ontological Argument
    Teleological Argument

Theology Proper

See:
Attributes of God
Decrees of God
Eternity
Freedom
Goodness
Holiness
Immutability
Justice
Love
Mercy
Names of God
Omnipotence
Omnipresence
Omniscience
Predestination
Sovereignty
Theism
Trinitarianism
Truthfulness
Wisdom

Thought Life

Time Management

Tithe
    See:
    Offerings
    Stewardship

TJTA, Instruments (Taylor-
    Johnson Temperament
    Analysis)

TJTA, Interpretation

Tongues

Topical Research (Teaching
    Method)

Tracts

See:
Evangelism Literature

Transfiguration

Translations

Trinitarianism

Trustees

Trustees, Potential

Truthfulness

Types & Symbols of the
    Holy Spirit
    See:
    Pneumatology

U

Unification Church (cult)

Unity

Universalism

Unlimited Atonement
    Use: Limited/Unlimited
        Atonement

Unsaved Spouse

V

Vacation Bible School, 1992
    Records

Vacation Bible School, 1993
    Records

Vacation Bible School,
    Administration

Vacation Bible School,
    Bibliography

Vacation Bible School,
    Bulletin Inserts

Vacation Bible School,
    Classes

Vacation Bible School,
    Correspondence

Vacation Bible School,
    Crafts

Vacation Bible School,
    Dedication Service

Vacation Bible School,
    Follow-Up Letter

Vacation Bible School,
    Ideas

Vacation Bible School, Job
    Descriptions

Vacation Bible School,
    Junior High

Vacation Bible School,
    Newspaper Ads

Vacation Bible School,
    Parents Night

Vacation Bible School,
    Planning Meeting
    Invitation Letter

Vacation Bible School,
    Preschool

Vacation Bible School,
    Primary

Vacation Bible School,
    Promotion

Vacation Bible School,
    Recommendations
    from Last Year

Vacation Bible School,
    Records

Vacation Bible School,
    Remarks

Vacation Bible School,
    Sources

Vacation Bible School,
    Training Seminar

Vacation Bible School,
    Unchurched Parents

Vacation Bible School,
    Unchurched Parents
    Invitation Letter

Vacation Bible School,
    Workers' Appreciation
    Letter

Vacation Bible School,
    Youth Volunteers

Virgin Birth
    See: Incarnation

Visitation
    See:
    Neighborhood Strategy

Visitation, Materials

Visitation, Member Strategy

Volunteer Leaders

W

War

Warranties

Wealth
    Use: Money

Wedding
    Use: Marriage

Widowhood
  See:
  Death, Acceptance of
      Another's
  Marriage

Wills

Wisdom

Witnessing
  Use: Evangelism

Women
  See:
  Feminism

Women, Role in the Church

Women, Role in the Family

Work Problems

Worker Recognition Day

Worry/Anxiety

Worship

Worship Attendance
    Records

X

Y

Youth
  See:
  Adolescence
  Specific ministries &
      topics

Youth Ministry Activities

Z

A Sample of a Topic-Subtopic Filing System

9

By way of review from chapter 3, the structure of a topic-subtopic or outline filing system is based on the three tabs that standard file folders have (left tab, middle tab, right tab). The organization of a filing system and its correspondence to an outline system follows. Note that the file drawer is considered to be the broadest level of organization. Thus, there are as many as four levels of organization available to the user.

Chart 9

Organi-zational level	Broadest category	Broad category	Narrow category	Narrowest category
	(Level one)	(Level two)	(Level three)	(Level four)
Outline indicator	I (Roman numerals)	A (Upper case letters)	1 (Arabic numerals)	a (Lower case letters)
Filing indicator	File drawer	Left cut/tab	Middle cut/tab	Right cut/tab

In this chapter, the three columns correspond to the three cuts of the file folders. The broadest category level (file drawer) will be indicated by a title in an outlined box, representing the metal frame on the outside of the file drawer into which a card with the title is placed. Broad categories (left-cut folders) are indicated by being the left column and are in bold italic letters. Narrow categories (middle-cut folders) are in the middle column and are in normal or Roman letters. Narrowest categories (right-cut folders) are in the right column and are in italic letters.

The major sections (broadest categories) of this filing system are as follows. (discussed in chapter 3)

Bible   General   Ministry   Personal   Theology

The following listing is a sample of a topic-subtopic filing system. All of the files in this system can be found organized as a separately indexed system in chapter 8.

GENERAL

Archeology

  Babylon
  Israel

Art

Apostasy

Books

  Reviews
  To Purchase List

Church History

  American
  Early
  Medieval
  Reformation

Dreams

Friendship

Languages

  Greek
      Grammar Notes
      Verb Charts
      Vocabulary Lists
  Hebrew
      Grammar Notes
      Verb Charts
      Vocabulary Lists
  Latin
      Grammar Notes
      Verb Charts
      Vocabulary Lists
  Spanish
      Grammar Notes
      Verb Charts
      Vocabulary Lists

Leadership

Martyrdom

Messages, Topical

  AAA Individual Message Title
  BBB Series Title
      Message #1 Title
      Message #2 Title

CCC Individual Message Title
DDD Individual Message Title
EEE Series Title
    Message #1 Title
    Message #2 Title
FFF Individual Message Title
GGG Series Title
    Message #1 Title
    Message #2 Title

Money

Parachurch Ministries

  AWANA
  Bible Societies
  Campus Crusade
  CBMC
  InterVarsity
  Navigators

Philosophy

**Religions, Christian Denominations/
  Groups**

      Baptist
      Brethren
      Charismatics
      Christian & Missionary
        Alliance
      Christian Science
      Episcopal
      Evangelical Free
      Evangelical Movement
      Fundamentalism
      Jehovah's Witness
      Lutheran
      Mennonite
      Methodist
      Pentecostal
      Presbyterian
      Seventh Day Adventist
      Roman Catholic
      Vineyard Movement

Religions, Non-Christian

  Animism
  Atheism
  Bahai
  Buddhism
  Confucianism
      Ancestor Worship

Hinduism
Idolatry
Islam
Judaism
Mormonism
New Age Movement
Shintoism
Taoism
Unification Church
Unity

Sacrifice

Translations

MINISTRY

Administration

Job Descriptions (Committee Level)
Organizational Chart
Robert's Rules of Order

Adults

Needs
Socials
Trends

Annual Meeting

Checklist
Report, 1992
Report, 1993

Audio Visuals

Catalogs
   Films
   Tapes
Committee
Equipment Manuals
   Movie Projector
   Slide Projector
   Tape Recorders
   VCR
Overhead Projector Masters
   Bible Geography
   Life of Christ
Slide Library Index
Tape Library Index

Baby Dedication

Ceremony
Certificates
Records

Baptism

Certificates
Committee Job Description
Handout for Prospect
Modes
Policies and Procedures
Records

Benevolence

Committee Records
Policies

Bible Study Methods

Buildings and Grounds

Committee
Facilities
   Building Plans
   Maintenance
      Agreements
Rental Agreements and Policies

Camping

Family Camp
   Camp Alwaysrains
   Camp Lotsabugs
   Child Care
   Programs, Adult
   Programs, General
   Programs, Youth
   Promotional Ideas
   Recreation Ideas
   Worship Ideas
Summer Youth Camp
   Camp Faraway
   Camp Terriblefood
   Programs
   Promotional Ideas
   Recreation Ideas
   Worship Ideas

Children

Needs
Trends

Christian Education Board
    Duties (Job Description)
    Minutes
    Policies

Christian Schools
    Local Elementary School
        Literature
    Regional High School
        Literature
    Seminaries

Church
    Constitution
    History
    Organizational Chart
    Directory

Church Picnic
    Committee Minutes
    Job Descriptions
    Schedule

Community Service
    Blood Drive
    Crisis Pregnancy Center
    Inner-City Mission
    Jail Ministry
    Poor
    Retirement Home Ministry
    Senior Servants Ministry

Conferences
    Bible Conferences
    Christian Education
    Counseling
    Marriage

Correspondence
    Church Related, 1992
    Church Related, 1993
    Counseling, 1992
    Counseling, 1993

Counseling
    Bibliography
    Aging Issues
        Health Needs
        Retirement
        Senility
        Widowhood

        Wills
    Childbearing Issues
        Abortion
        Adoption
        Artificial
            Insemination
        Birth Control
        Infertility
        Pregnancy,
            Unmarried
        Pregnancy,
            Unwanted/
            Unplanned
        Sterility
    Childrearing Issues
        Blended Family
        Child Abuse
        Handicapped Child
        Rebellious Child
        Single Parenting
    General Issues
        Celibacy
        Death, Acceptance of
            Another's
        Death, Acceptance of
            Own
        Decision Making &
            the Will of God
        Divorce
        Doubtful Things
        Fighting, Rules for
        Gossip
        Mental Illness,
            General Types of
        Pain & Suffering
        Procrastination
        Self-Discipline
        Sickness
        Stress
        Suicide
        Television
        Thought Life
        Time Management
        Unsaved Spouse
        Work Problems
    Personal Issues
        Anger/Temper
        Depression
        Fear

Greed
Guilt
Inferiority
Loneliness
Lying
Worry/Anxiety
Referral Sources
Hospitals
Individuals
Organizations
Resources
Seminar Notes, 6/92
Sexual Issues
Adultery
Homosexuality
Incest
Masturbation
Pornography
Substance Abuse Issues
Alcoholism
Drugs
Tests
TJTA, Instruments
TJTA, Interpretation

Discipleship

Devotional Life
Aids for
Bible Reading
Schedules
Meditation
Seminar Notes
Fasting
Follow-Up of New Believers
Materials
Bible Study
Fellowship
Campus Crusade
Churches Alive
Navigators
Prayer
Church List
Lord's Prayer
Personal List
Unanswered,
Response to
Renewal of Recommited
Believers
Small Groups

Discipline, Church

Emergency & Disaster Plans

Evacuation Plan
Notification Plan

Ethical Issues

Abortion
AIDS
Crime & Punishment
Capital Punishment
Euthanasia
Gambling
War

Evangelism

Bibliography
Child Evangelism Fellowship
Good News Clubs
Committee Notes
Strategy for Anytown
Gospel Presentations
Evangelism
Explosion
Four Spiritual Laws
Roman Road
Neighborhood Evangelistic
Bible Studies
Bible Discussion
Notes
"Inviting Your
Neighbor"
handouts
Literature
Samples
Sources

Family Night

Ideas
Board Game Night
Kids vs Parents Quiz
Show
Super Bowl Sunday
Schedule, Current Year
Records, Previous Years

Funerals

Ceremony
Music Selections
Scriptures

Cremation
Records

Home

Bibliography
Discipline
Parents, Role of
Spiritual Training of Children

Lord's Supper

Ceremony
Committee Job Description
Policies and Procedures
Record of Services
Scripture Readings

Marriage (Also see Counseling)

Bibliography
Ceremonies
Music
Service Outlines
Records
Divorce
Engagement Studies
Adjusting
Emotionally
Adjusting
Financially
Adjusting Physically
Adjusting Spiritually
Ceremony Ideas
(poems, songs,
and so forth)
Honeymoon
Legal Issues
Parenthood
Sexual Issues

Membership

Application Form
Doctrinal Statement
Lists
Active
Discipline
Inactive
Mailings Only

Missions

Annual Conference
Job Descriptions

Speakers
Participating
Mission Agencies
Supporting Agencies &
Individuals
Agency
Individual
Policies
Candidacy Materials

Music

Bibliography
Choirs
Children
Junior
Adult
Committee
Equipment
Instruments
Music
Robes
Hymns

Newsletter

Current Issue
Ideas
1992
1993

Officers

Elders
Annual Report
Job Description
Minutes
Potential Elders
Deacons
Annual Report
Job Description
Minutes
Potential Deacons
Trustees
Annual Report
Budget
Job Description
Minutes
Potential Trustees
Stewardship
Campaign Ideas

Ordination

Ceremony
Records

Policies

Publicity

Bulletin Board Ideas
Bulletin Insert Ideas
Church Brochure
Sample Brochures
Committee
Annual Report
Job Description
Minutes
"I Need Publicity" Forms
Newspaper Ads
Sample Ads

Records

Giving
Sunday School Attendance
Worship Attendance

Resumé

Schedule

Sex Education

Adolescence
Articles
Bibliography
Home Responsibilities

Special Dates (anniversaries, birthdays, and so forth)

January
February
March
April
May
June
July
August
September
October
November
December

Special Days

Advent
Ascension

Christmas
Easter
Evangelistic
Father's Day
Good Friday
Graduation
Lent
Mother's Day
Pentecost
Thanksgiving
Worker Recognition

Staff

Retreat
Devotionals
Planning Sheets
Personal Information
Potential Personnel

Stewardship

Bulletin Ideas
Materialism
Personal
Budgeting
Wills

Sunday School

Adult Department
Classes
Curriculum
Potential Workers
Schedule
Awards Catalogs
Children's Church
Primary
Junior
Children, Nature & Needs
Infants (0-2)
Nursery (2-3)
Kindergarten (4-5)
Primary (6-8)
College Department
Classes
Curriculum
Potential Workers
Schedule
Convention, 1992
Convention, 1993
Convention, 199–
Evaluation

Department
Student
Teacher
Facilities
Floor Plans
Setup Requirements
Junior High Department
Classes
Curriculum
Potential Workers
Schedule
Mission Sunday
Ideas
Schedule
Moving-Up Day
Awards
Job Descriptions
Parent Letters & Take
Homes
Schedule
Nursery Department
Potential Workers
Schedule
Visitation Materials
Policy Handbook
Primary Department
Classes
Curriculum
Potential Workers
Schedule
Puppet Ministry
Senior High Department
Classes
Curriculum
Potential Workers
Schedule
Single Adult Department
Classes
Curriculum
Potential Workers
Schedule
Staff
Department Heads
Secretary
Organizational Chart
Supplies (markers, paper, and
so forth)
Inventory
Order Records

Catalogs
Teacher Job Descriptions
Teacher Training Day
Evaluations
Future Ideas
Materials
Process of Teaching
Schedule
Teaching Methods (How-to
handouts)
Debate
Demonstration
Discussion
Dramatization
Forum
Lecture
Memorization
Panel
Problem Solving
Projects
Question & Answer
Role Playing
Storytelling
Topical research

Tabernacle

Vacation Bible School
Administration
Job Descriptions
Schedule
Bibliography
Classes
Preschool
Primary
Junior High
Correspondence
Planning Meeting
Invitation Letter
Unchurched Parents
Follow-Up Letter
Unchurched Parents
Invitation Letter
Worker's
Appreciation
Letter
Crafts
Ideas
Sources
Dedication Service

Schedule
Remarks
Parents' Night
Promotion
   Bulletin Inserts
   Newspaper Ads
   Recommendations
     from Last Year
Records
   1992 Records
   1993 Records
Youth Volunteers
   Training Seminar
   Job Description

Visitation

Member Strategy
Neighborhood Strategy
Surveys
Training Program

Wednesday Service

Prayer Lists
Message Ideas

Women

Role in the Church
Role in the Family
Feminism

Worship

Benedictions
Bulletin File, 1992
Bulletin File, 1993
Current Month Plan
Ideas for Future
Master Calendar of Sunday
   Service Themes and
   Messages
Sunday Morning Service
   Worksheets
Sunday Evening Service
   Worksheets

Youth Ministry

Activities
AWANA
Bible Studies
Dating
Needs
Socials

Trends
Volunteer Leaders
Youth Minister
   Job Description

PERSONAL

Auto Title

Computer

Warranties

Correspondence

Personal, 1992
Personal, 1993

Education

College Records
Seminary Records

Finances

Bank Statements
   1992
   1993
Budget
   1992
   1993

Goals

Current Personal
Current Family
Previous

Health Records

Self
Spouse
Child

Insurance

Auto
Health
House
Life

Manuals & Warranties

Appliances
Tools

Tax Records

Federal Income
1992
1993
Sales
1992
1993
State Income
1992
1993

Travel

THEOLOGY

Angelology

Angels, Good
Occult
Satan & Demons

Anthropology

Eden, Prefall State
Harmatology
The Fall
Original Sin
Seven Deadly Sins
Image of God
Soul

Apologetics

Astrology
Bibliography
Evolution
Miracles
Theistic Arguments
Cosmological
Argument
Teleological
Argument
Anthropological
Argument
Ontological
Argument

Biblical Theology

Old Testament Theology
New Testament Theology
Johannine Theology
Pauline Theology

Petrine Theology

Bibliology

Canonicity & Authority
Covenant Theology
Dispensational Theology
Illumination
Inspiration
Interpretation
(Hermeneutics)
Revelation, General
Revelation, Special
Inerrancy

Christology

Deity
Offices
Incarnation
Ascension
Baptism
Death
Resurrection
Transfiguration
Virgin Birth

Ecclesiology

Church Local (Organization)
Polity
Offices
Church Universal (Organism)
Ordinances
Baptism
Foot Washing
Lord's Table

Eschatology

Antichrist
Eternal State
Heaven
Hell
Historical Survey
Judgment
Messianic Prophecy
Millennium
Amillennialism
Postmillennialism
Premillennialism
Rapture

Historical Theology (see also Church History)

Pneumatology

> Types & Symbols of the Holy
>   Spirit
> Indwelling
> Baptizing
> Sealing
> Filling
> Fruit
> Gifts
> Tongues

Prolegomena

> Science
> > *Creationism*
> > * /Evolution*
>
> Heresies (Antitheistic)
> > *Agnosticism*
> > *Humanism*
> > *Liberation Theology*
> > *Materialism*
> > *Polytheism*

Sanctification

Soteriology

> Atonement
> > *Limited/Unlimited*
>
> Faith
> Gospel
> Grace
> Lordship Salvation
> Redemption
> Repentance
> Salvation

> *Assurance of*
> * Justification*
> *Sanctification*
> *Glorification*
> *Universalism*

Theology Proper

> Attributes of God
> > *Eternity*
> > *Freedom*
> > *Goodness*
> > *Holiness*
> > *Immutability*
> > *Justice*
> > *Love*
> > *Mercy*
> > *Omnipotence*
> > *Omnipresence*
> > *Omniscience*
> > *Personality*
> > *Sovereignty*
> > *Truthfulness*
> > *Wisdom*
>
> Decrees of God
> > *Predestination*
>
> Names of God
> > *Old Testament*
> > *New Testament*
>
> Theism
> Trinitarianism

A Sample of a Filing System for Bible-Related Materials

The following is a suggested format for Book of the Bible files[1]. This section is discussed in detail in chapter 4. Users will note that in addition to Bible material on a particular book or passage, this section of the file contains other materials directly related to the study of the Bible.

The following section has three columns. Each column uses indentation to represent left, middle and right cut folders. Each book of the Bible uses a left cut folder, major divisions of the book use a middle cut folder, and individual study units for preaching or teaching use a right cut folder.

The only exception to this pattern is for the Gospels. The filing of them is based on the overlap of subject matter in the Gospels. The system offers two possibilities. First, make up numbered folders as indicated in the far left column. Second, file in another manner and use the outline as a guide to cross-referencing.

Bible

N.T. Character Studies
N.T. Word Studies
  Word α
  Word β
O.T. Character Studies
O.T. Word Studies
  Word א
  Word ד

---

1. The author is indebted to Dr. Donald Sunukjian for the divisions used here with some revision.

Genesis

1–11
  1–2
  3
  4–5
  6–9
  10–11
12–26
  12–17
  18–20
  21–22
  23–26
27–36
  27–30
  31–33
  34–36
37–50
  37–38
  39–41
  42–47
  48–50

Exodus

1–11
  1–4
  5–11
12–18
  12–15
  16–18
19–24
  19–20
  21–24
25–31
32–40
  32–34
  35–40

Leviticus

1–10
  1–7
  8–10
11–27
  11–16
  17–27

Numbers

1–12
  1–6
  7–12

13–20
  13–14
  15–20
21–36
  21–25
  26–32
  33–36

Deuteronomy

1–11
  1–4
  5–7
  8–11
12–34
  12–16
  17–21
  22–26
  27–30
  31–34

Joshua

1–5
  1–2
  3–5
6–12
  6–8
  9–10
  11–12
13–24
  13–22
  23–24

Judges

1–5
  1–2
  3–5
6–12
  6–9
  10–12
13–21
  13–16
  17–21

Ruth

Entire Book

1 Samuel

1–12
  1–3
  4–7
  8–12
13–31
  13–15
  16–20
  21–27
  28–31

2 Samuel

1–10
  1–4
  5–10
11–24
  11–12
  13–19
  20–24

1 Kings

1–11
  1–4
  5–11
12–22
  12–16
  17–19
  20–22

2 Kings

1–8
  1–3
  4–8
9–17
  9–12
  13–17
18–25
  18–21
  22–25

I Chronicles

1–9
10–20
  10–14
  15–20

21–29

2 Chronicles

1–9
10–24
  10–16
  17–24
25–36
  25–28
  29–33
  34–36

Ezra

1–6
7–10

Nehemiah

1–7
8–13

Esther

Entire Book

Job

1–14
  1–2
  3–14
15–31
  15–21
  22–31
32–42
  32–37
  38–42

Psalms

Each Psalm

Proverbs

1–9
10–24
  10–22
  23–24
25–31
  25–29
  30–31

Ecclesiates

- 1–6
- 7–12

Song of Solomon

Entire Book

Isaiah

- 1–12
  - 1–6
  - 7
  - 8–12
- 13–39
  - 13–35
  - 36–39
- 40–48
  - 40–41
  - 42–48
- 49–57
  - 49–52
  - 53
  - 54–57
- 58–66

Jeremiah

- 1–20
- 1
- 2–10
- 11–20
- 21–39
  - 21–29
  - 30–33
  - 34–36
  - 37–39
- 40–52
  - 40–45
  - 46–51
  - 52

Lamentations

Entire Book

Ezekiel

- 1–24
  - 1–3
  - 4–11
  - 12–24
- 25–48
  - 25–32
  - 33–39
  - 40–48

Daniel

- 1–6
  - 1
  - 2
  - 3
  - 4
  - 5
  - 6
- 7–12
  - 7
  - 8
  - 9
  - 10–12

Hosea

- 1–3
- 4–14

Joel

Entire Book

Amos

Entire Book

Obadiah

Entire Book

Jonah

Entire Book

Micah

Entire Book

Nahum

Entire Book

Habakkuk

Entire Book

Zephaniah

Entire Book

Haggai

Entire Book

Zechariah

- 1–6
- 7–14

Malachi

Entire Book

Matthew	Mark	Luke	John
1			1:1–18
2	1:1–17	3:23–38	
3		1:5–25	
4		1:26–38	
5		1:39–56	
6		1:57–80	
7	1:18–25		
8		2:1–20	
9		2:21–40	
10	2:1–23		

	Matthew	Mark	Luke	John
11			2:41–52	
12	3:1–12	1:1–8	3:1–20	
13	3:13–17	1:9–11	3:21–32	
14	4:1–11	1:12–13	4:1–13	
15				1:19–34
16				1:35–42
17				1:43–51
18				2:1–11
19				2:12–22
20				2:23–3:21
21				3:22–36
22				4:1–42
23				4:43–54
24			4:14–32	
25	4:12–17			
26	4:18–22	1:14–20		
27		1:21–28	4:31–37	
28	8:14–17	1:29–34	4:38–41	
29	4:23–25	1:35–39	4:42–44	
30			5:1–11	
31	5:1–12			
32	5:13–16			
33	5:17–48			
34	6:1–18			
35	6:19–34			
36	7:1–6			
37	7:7–12			
38	7:13–29			
39	8:1–4	1:40–45	5:12–16	
40	9:1–8	2:1–2	5:17–26	
41	9:9–13	2:13–17	5:27–32	
42	9:14–17	2:18–22	5:33–39	
43				5:1–47
44	12:1–8	2:23–38	6:1–5	
45	12:9–21	3:1–12	6:6–11	
46		3:13–19	6:12–19	
47			6:20–27	
48			6:28–36	
49			6:37–42	
50			6:43–49	

	Matthew	Mark	Luke	John
51	8:5–13		7:1–10	
52			7:11–17	
53	11:2–19		7:18–35	
54	11:20–24			
55	11:25–30			
56			7:36–50	
57	12:22–45	3:20–30		
58	12:46–50	3:31–35	8:18–21	
59	13:1–23	4:1–25	8:1–18	
60		4:26–29		
61	13:24–52	4:30–34	13:18–21	
62	8:18, 23–27	4:35–41	8:22–25	
63	8:28–34	5:1–20	8:26–39	
64	9:18–26	5:21–43	8:40–56	
65	9:27–38			
66	13:53–58	6:1–6		
67	10:1–11:1	6:7–13	9:1–6	
68	14:1–12	6:14–29	9:7–9	
69	14:13–21	6:30–44	9:10–17	6:1–13
70	14:22–36	6:45–56		6:14–21
71				6:22–71
72	15:1–20	7:1–23		
73	15:21–28	7:24–30		
74		7:31–37		
75	15:29–39	8:1–10		
76	16:1–4	8:11–13		
77	16:5–12	8:14–21		
78		8:22–26		
79	16:13–28	8:27–9:1	9:18–27	
80	17:1–8	9:2–8	9:28–36	
81	17:9–13	9:9–13		
82	17:14–21	9:14–29	9:37–43	
83	17:22–23	9:30–32	9:43–45	
84	17:24–27			
85	18:1–14	9:35–50	9:46–50	
86	18:15–35			
87				7:1–10
88			9:51–56	
89	8:19–22		9:57–62	
90				7:11–52

Matthew	Mark	Luke	John
91			7:53–8:11
92			8:12–20
93			8:21–59
94			9:1–41
95			10:1–21
96		10:1–24	
97		10:25–37	
98		10:38–42	
99		11:1–13	
100		11:14–36	
101		11:37–54	
102		12:1–34	
103		12:35–59	
104		13:1–9	
105		13:10–17	
106			10:22–42
107		13:22–35	
108		14:1–24	
109		14:25–35	
110		15:1–32	
111		16:1–18	
112		16:19–31	
113		17:1–10	
114			11:1–44
115			11:45–54
116		17:11–19	
117		17:20–37	
118		18:1–8	
119		18:9–14	
120	19:1–12	10:1–12	
121	19:13–15	10:13–16	18:15–17
122	19:16–20:16		18:18–30
123	20:17–28	10:17–31	18:31–34
124	20:29–34	10:32–45	18:35–43
125		10:46–52	19:1–10
126			19:11–28
127			11:55–12:11
128	21:1–22	11:1–26	19:29–48	12:12–19
129				12:20–50
130	21:23–32	11:27–33	20:1–8	

	Matthew	Mark	Luke	John
131	21:33–46	12:1–12	20:9–19	
132	22:1–14			
133	22:15–22	12:13–17	20:20–26	
134	22:23–40	12:18–34	20:27–40	
135	22:41–46	12:35–37	20:41–44	
136	23:1–39	12:38–44	20:45–21:4	
137	24:1–25:46	13:1–37	21:5–38	
138	26:1–16	14:1–11	22:1–6	
139	26:17–19	14:12–16	22:7–13	
140				13:1–20
141	26:20–29	14:17–25	22:14–30	13:21–30
142	26:30–35	15:26–31	22:31–38	13:31–38
143				14:1–31
144				15:1–17
145				15:18–27
146				16:1–11
147				16:12–33
148				17:1–26
149	26:36–46	14:32–42	22:39–46	
150	26:47–56	14:43–52	22:47–53	18:1–11
151	26:57–75	14:53–72	22:54–65	18:12–27
152	27:1–26	15:1–15	22:66–23:25	18:28–19:16a
153	27:27–44	15:16–32	23:26–43	19:16b–27
154	27:45–56	15:33–41	23:44–49	19:28–37
155	27:57–66	15:42–47	23:50–56	19:38–42
156	28:1–15	16:1–11	24:1–12	20:1–18
157		16:12–13	24:13–35	
158		16:14	24:36–43	20:19–31
159				21:1–25
160	28:16–20	16:15–18		
161		16:19–20	24:44–53	

Acts

1–7	6:1–7:60	13:1–14:28	19:21–41
	8–12	15:1–35	20:1–21:14
1:1–26	8:1–40	15:36–16:5	21:15–23:35
2:1–42	9:1–31	16:6–40	24:1–26:32
2:43–47	9:32–43	17:1–15	27:1–28:31
3:1–4:4	10:1–11:18	17:16–34	
4:5–31	11:19–30	18:1–23	**Romans**
4:32–5:11	12:1–25	19–28	1–3
5:12–42	13–18	18:24–19:20	1:1–17

1:18–32
2:1–3:8
3:9–31
4–5
4:1–25
5:1–11
5:12–21
6–8
6:1–23
7:1–25
8:1–39
9–11
12–16
12:1–21
13:1–14
14:1–15:13
15:14–16:27

1 Corinthians

1–4
1:1–17
1:18–2:5
2:6–3:4
3:5–4:5
4:6–21
5–6
5:1–13
6:1–11
6:12–20
7
8–11
8
9
10:1–13
10:14–11:1
11:2–16
11:17–34
12–14
12
13
14
15–16
15
16

2 Corinthians

1–7
1:1–11
1:12–2:4
2:5–13
2:14–3:6
3:7–4:6
4:7–15
4:16–5:10
5:11–6:10

6:11–7:1
7:2–16
8–9
8:1–15
8:16–24
9
10–13
10
11
12:1–10
12:11–21
13

Galatians

1–2
1:1–10
1:11–24
2:1–10
2:11–21
3
3:1–9
3:10–22
3:23–29
4–6
4:1–7
4:8–20
4:21–5:1
5:2–12
5:13–26
6:1–10
6:11–18

Ephesians

1–3
1:1–14
1:15–23
2:1–10
2:11–22
3:1–13
3:14–21
4–6
4:1–16
4:17–5:2
5:3–21
5:22–33
6:1–9
6:10–24

Philippians

1
1:1–11
1:12–30
2
2:1–11
2:12–18

2:19–30
3
3:1–16
3:17–4:1
4
4:2–9
4:10–23

Colossians

1
1:1–8
1:9–23
1:24–2:5
2
2:6–19
2:20–3:4
3
3:5–17
3:18–4:1
4
4:2–6
4:7–18

1 Thessalonians

1–3
1:1–10
2:1–12
2:13–3:5
3:6–13
4–5
4:1–12
4:13–18
5:1–11
5:12–28

2 Thessalonians

1
2
3

1 Timothy

1
1:1–11
1:12–20
2
3
3:1–7
3:8–16
4
5
5:1–15
5:17–25
6
6:1–10

6:11–21

2 Timothy

1
2
2:1–13
2:14–26
3
3:1–9
3:10–17
4
4:1–8
4:9–22

Titus

1
1:1–9
1:10–16
2
2:1–10
2:11–15
3
3:1–7
3:8–15

Philemon

Entire Book

Hebrews

1–4
1:1–2:4
2:5–18
3:1–4:13
5–10
4:14–5:10
5:11–6:20
7
8
9:1–10:18
10:19–39
11–13
11
12
13

James

1
1:1–18
1:19–27
2
2:1–13
2:14–26
3

4
  3:1–12
  3:13–18
  4:1–12
  4:13–5:6
5
  5:7–12
  5:13–20

1 Peter
1
  1:1–12
  1:13–21
  1:22–25
2
  2:1–10
  2:11–12
  2:13–17
  2:18–25

3
  3:1–7
  3:8–12
  3:13–4:6
4
  4:7–11
  4:12–19
5
  5:1–5
  5:6–14

2 Peter
1
  1:1–11
  1:12–21
2
3

1 John
1
2
  2:1–17
  2:18–29
3
  3:1–9
  3:10–24
4
  4:1–6
  4:7–21
5
  5:1–12
  5:13–21

2 John
  Entire Book

3 John
  Entire Book

Jude
  Entire Book

Revelation
1–3
  1:1–20
  2:1–3:22
4–11
  4:1–5:14
  6:1–8:1
  8:2–11:19
12–18
  12:1–14:20
  15:1–18:24
19–22

A Sample of a Filing System for Illustrations

The adoption of the following listing of topics for filing illustrations will provide for consistency in filing illustrations, simplicity of filing and retrieving so that others can file illustrations for you, and flexibility because room has been left for additional topics and cross-references to be added.

Two terms are used in this index of topics. The term *See* means that the following topic(s) are related to the topic at hand and may be worth examining. The term *Use* means that the following topic is so close in meaning to the one at hand that it should be used instead.

The following terms can be used to narrow most topics. The use of a standardized list of terms for narrowing topics makes it easier to quickly find the illustration you want. Thus, the following common terms are not included in the list of topics for filing illustrations.

Application of
Benefit of
Effect of
Example of
Definition/Description of
Humorous
Lack of
Motive for

Necessity of
Purpose for
Requirements for
Results/Consequences of
Response to
Source of
Value of

A

Abiding

Ability

Abortion

Absolutes

Absolution
  Use: Forgiveness

Abstinence
  See: Addiction

Accidents

Adam

Addiction
  See: Abstinence;
  Alcoholism; Drugs

Administration
  See: Government

Admonish
  Use: Warning

Adolescence
  Use: Youth

Adoption
  of children
  spiritual

Adultery
  See: Fornication; Sex

Advent

Adversity
  See: Problems

Advice

Affection

Affliction
  See: Adversity; Problem;
  Testing; Trials

Age

Aging

Agnosticism
  See: Unbelief

Alcohol

Alcoholism
  See: Abstinence

Allurement
  Use: Temptation

Altar
  See: Worship; Call; Family;
  Old Testament

Ancestor Worship

Angel
  See: Devil; Satan

Anger
  See: Temper; Wrath

Anniversary

Antichrist

Antimony

Anxiety
  See: Fear; Worry

Apathy

Apologetics

Apology

Apostate
  See: Doctrine, False

Apostasy

Approval

Arguments

Armageddon

Arminianism
  See: Free Will

Art

Asceticism
  See: Celibacy; Fasting

Assumptions

Assurance of Salvation
  Use: Salvation, Assurance
  of

Astrology

Atheism
  See: Agnosticism;
  Apologetics; Unbelief

Atonement
  See: Christ, Death;
  Expiation; Propitiation;
  Substitution, Example of

Attendance
  Use; Church Attendance

Attitudes
  See: Optimism;
  Pessimism; (Various
  character traits)

Attributes of God
  Use: God, (name of
  attribute)

Authority, of Bible
  See: Bible, Authority of

Avarice
  Use: Greed

Awe
  Use: Reverence

B

Baby
  Dedication
    Use: Dedication, Baby

Bachelor

Backbiting
  Use: Gossip

Banquet

Baptism

Beatitudes

Beauty

Behavior, Inconsistent

Belief
  Use: Faith

Bible
  Authority of
  Belief in
  Context,
    Importance of
  Effects of Reading
  Hatred of
  Illumination of
  Inspiration of
  Interpretation of
    Use: Hermeneutics
  Inerrancy of
  Knowledge of
  Necessity of Reading
  Problem Passages
  Reliability of
  Study of
  Translations

Bigamy

Birth, of Baby

Birth, of Christ
  Use: Christ, Incarnation;
  or Christmas

Birth, New
  Use: Regeneration

Bishops
  See: Church, Leaders

Bitterness
  Use: Resentment

Blasphemy
  See: Cursing; Swearing

Blessings

Blindness, Spiritual

Blood of Christ
  Use: Christ, Blood of

Boasting
  See: Pride

Body of Christ
  Use: Church

Boys
  Use: Children, Boys

Bride
  Use: Church, Bride of
  Christ; or Marriage

Buddhism

Budget
  See: Money; Stewardship

Burdens
  Use: Adversity; Problems

C

Calamity

Call

Calvary
  See: Substitution

Calvinism

Capital Punishment

Capitalism

Celebration

Carnality

Celibacy

Chance
  See: Gambling

Change

Character
  Use:(name of specific
  character trait)
  Test of

Charismata
  See: Tongues

Cheating

Child-rearing
  See: Children; Discipline

Children
  Boys
  Death of
  Desire to Please Parents
  Evangelism to
  Faith of
  Girls
  Mothering
  Need for Affection
    Use: Affection,
    Need for
  Prayers
    Use: Prayer
  Play
  Sinfulness of
    Use: Sin

Choices

Christie
  Body of
    Use: Church
  Blood of
  Crucified,
  the Gospel of
    Use: Gospel
  Death of
    Use: Substitution
  Deity of
  Identification with
  Impeccability of
  Incarnation
  Miracles of
    See: Miracles, of Christ
  Resurrection of
    See: Resurrection, of Christ
  Return of
  Statements about
  Sufficiency of
  Union with

Christian

Christian Home

Christian Liberty
  Use: Liberty, Christian

Christian Life
  See: Sanctification; Trials; Worldliness
  Failure in
  Growth in
  Knowing God
  Living It
  Witness of
    Use: Witness

Christianity

Christmas

Church
  Attendance
  Bride of Christ
  Discipline
  Finances
  Involvement
  Leaders of

Love
  Mission of
  Membership
  Separation
    Use: Separation
  Service to
  Size of
  Strife within
  Unity of
  World's Perspective of

Circumcision

Circumstances

Citizenship

Civilization

Clergy
  Use: Minister

College

Comfort

Commandments
  See: Ten Commandments

Commencement
  Use: Graduation

Commitment
  See: Commitment; Dedication; Marriage; Obedience

Common Grace
  Use: Grace, Common

Communion
  Use: Lord's Supper

Communism

Compassion
  See: Love; Mercy; Sympathy

Complaining

Complaints

Compromise

Conceit
  See: Pride

Concern

Conclusions

Conferences

Confession

Confirmation

Conformity

Conscience
  Clear
  Guilty

Contentment

Consequences

Consecration

Consolation
  Use: Comfort

Conversion
  See: Regeneration
  Process of

Conviction, of sin
  Use: Sin, Conviction of

Convictions

Cooperation

Cost

Counseling
  See: Comfort

Country

Courage

Covenant

Covetousness
  See: Greed

Creation

Creationism

Creator

Crime

Crisis

Criticism
  Ignoring
  Positive

Cross

Crucifixion

Crowd

Cults

Cursing
  See: Swearing

D

Deacons

Deaconess

Death
  See: Comfort; Eternal Life;
  Immortality; Peace
  Believer's Response to
  Of a Child
  Fear of
  Last Words
  Ministry to
    Terminally Ill
  Mourning for
    See: Comfort
  Preparation for

Unbeliever's Response
  to

Debt
  Use: Money

Deceit
  Use: Lying

Deception

Decision

Dedication
  Baby
  Life

Deity
  Use: Christ, Deity of; God

Democracy

Demon
  Use: Devil
  See: Satan

Depravity
  Use: Sin

Depression
  See: Joy

Despair

Determination
  Use: Perseverance

Devil
  See: Satan

Diligence
  Use: Discipline;
  Faithfulness; Ministry,
  Preparing for; Perseverance

Disease
  See: Sickness

Disbelief

Disciple

Discipleship
  See: Commitment

Discipline
  See: Church, Discipline;
  Childrearing, Discipline;
  Diligence; Faithfulness;
  Ministry, Preparing for;
  Testing; Trials
  By God to Believers
    Use: Adversity,
    God's Use of
  Object of
  Self

Discouragement
  See: Character;
  Complaining;
  Encouragement;
  Determination
  Devil's use of

Disobedience

Dispensation

Disputes
  Use: Arguments

Divorce

Doctrine
  False
    See: Apostate
  Sound

Doubt
  See: Unbelief

Drinking;
  Use: Abstinence; or
  Alcohol; or Alcoholism

Drugs

Drunkenness
  Use: Abstinence; or
  Alcohol; or Alcoholism

Duty
  See: Commitment

Dying
Use: Death

E

Earth

Easter
*See: Resurrection, of
Christ*

Eating

Ecumenism

Economics

Edification
See: Encouragement

Education
Christian
Sex
Use: Sex, Education

Ego

Egotism

Elder
*See: Church, Leaders of;
Leader; Leadership;
Servant; Servanthood;
Service*

Election

Emotions

Employer
See: Work

Encouragement

Endurance
*See: Discipline;
Faithfulness; Perseverance*

Enemies

Entertainment

Enthusiasm
See: Zeal

Envy
See: Jealousy

Eschatology
See: Rapture

Eternal Death
Use: Hell

Eternal Life
See: Immortality

Eternal Perspective
See: Hope

Eternal Security

Euthanasia

Evangelism
*See: Apathy Conversion;
Missions; Procrastination;
Witness; Witnessing, Fear
In*
Boldness
Church
Clarity in
Commitment to
Methods

Evil
Existence of
Problem of

Evolution
See: Creation

Example

Excellence

Excuses

Exhortation

Experience

Expiation
*See: Atonement;
Propitiation*

F

Factions

Facts

Failure
See: Spiritual Growth

Faith
*See: Salvation;
Justification*
Acquiring of
Childlike
Content of
Development of
Exercise of
Fact and Feeling
and Law
Loss of
Object of
and Prayer
and Salvation
and Works

Faithfulness
*See: Discipline;
Endurance; God,
Faithfulness of;
Perseverance*

Fall (season of)

Fall, of Man

Fallen Angels
Use: Devils

False Gods
Use: Idolatry

Falsehood
Use: Lying

Fame
  See: Character

Family
  See: Children; Fathers;
  Childrearing; Discipline
  Christian, Benefits of
  Leadership in
  Spirituality
  Survival of

Fanatic

Fasting

Fatalism

Father

Father's Day

Faultfinding

Faults

Fear
  See: Anxiety; Worry

Fellowship

Fighting

Finances
  See: Greed; Money

Firstfruits

Fishing

Flattery

Flesh

Flood

Flying

Following

Food

Fool

Foolishness

Footwashing
  See: John 13:1-20

Forbearance
  Use: Patience

Force
  Use: Power

Forgetting

Forgiveness
  See: Salvation; Sin
  Acceptance of
  Basis of
  Forgetting Aspect of

Fornication
  See: Sex

Foundation, Importance of

Free will

Freedom

Friendship
  False
  True

Friends

Fruit of the Spirit

Frustration

Funerals

Future
  See: Eschatology

G

Gambling

Generosity

Gifts, Spiritual
  See: Spiritual Gifts

Girls
  Use: Children, Girls

Giving
  See: Money; Priorities;
  Tithing; Taxation
  Proportional
  Regular
  Selfishness in

Goals

God
  Arguing with
  Attributes of
    Use: God, (name of
    attribute)
    See: Grace; Mercy
  Blasphemous Statements
  Evidence of
  Faithfulness of
  Foreknowledge of
  Goodness of
  Glory of
  Immutability of
  Indivisibility of
  Invisible
  Knowing Him
  Longsuffering
    Use: Patience
  Love of
  Names of
  Omnipotence of
  Omnipresence of
  Omniscience of
  Patience of
  Providence of
  Righteousness of
  Sovereignty of
  Trinity
    Use: Trinity
  Trustworthiness of
  Will of
  Wrath of

Gods, False
  Use: Idolatry

Goliath

Golden Rule

Gospel
  See: Evangelism;
  Conversion; Grace;
  Election; Witness
  Call of
  Content of
  Minister of
  Power of

Gossip
  See: Tongue

Government

Grace
  See: Forgiveness; Law and
  Grace; Salvation, Gift of
  Common
  Efficacious
  False
  Irresistible

Grades

Graduation

Gratitude
  See: Ingratitude;
  Thankfulness

Great Commandment

Great Commission

Greatness

Greed
  See: Honesty; Selfishness

Grief
  See: Suffering

Grudges

Guidance
  See: Life, Purpose of; Will,
  of God

Guilt

H

Habits

Hades
  Use: Hell

Halloween

Happiness

Harlot

Harping
  See: Nagging

Hate

Hatred

Haughtiness
  Use: Pride

Head
  of the church
    Use: Christ; Church
  in marriage
    Use: Husband

Healing

Health

Heart
  See: Love
  New
    See: Regeneration

Heathen

Heaven

Hebrew

Hell
  See: Sheol
  Certainty of

Heresy
  See: Apostate; Doctrine,
  False

Hermeneutics
  See: Bible
  Context
  Relationship of OT to NT

Heroin

Hinduism

History

Holidays

Holiness
  of God
    Use: God, Holiness
    of
  of people
    See: Sanctification

Holy Spirit
  Filling
  Fruit of
    Use: Fruit of the
    Spirit
  Indwelling
  Ministry of
  Sealing of

Home Bible Studies

Home
  See: Family
  Christian

Homosexuality

Honesty
  See: Greed; Integrity

Honor

Hope
  See: Eternal Perspective
  False
  True

Hopelessness

Hospitality

Humanism

Humility

Humor

Hunger
  Physical
  Spiritual

Husband

Hymns

Hypocrisy

Hypocrite

I

Identification, with Christ

Idolatry

Ignorance
  See: Knowledge

Illness
  See: Sickness

Illumination
  Use: Bible, Illumination of

Image of God

Imitation

Immersion
  Use: Baptism

Immorality
  See: Fornication; Sex

Immortality
  See: Eternal Life

Impeccability
  Use: Christ, Impeccability of

Imputation
  of righteousness
    Use: Justification
  of sin
    Use: Sin, Imputation of

Inadequacy

Incarnation
  Use: Christ, Incarnation

Indifference

Indwelling
  Use: Holy Spirit, Indwelling

Inerrancy
  Use: Bible, Inerrancy

Infant
  Use: Baby

Infatuation

Infidelity
  See: Adultery; Immortality

Inflation (economic)

Ingratitude
  See: Gratitude

Inheritance

Iniquity
  See: Sin

Initiative

Insignificance

Inspiration
  Use, Bible, Inspiration of

Intelligence

Interpretation
  See: Hermeneutics

Irony

IRS
  See: Taxes

Islam

Ingratitude

Inspiration
  Use: Bible, Inspiration of

Integrity
  See: Greed; Honesty; Testing

Israel

J

Jealousy
  See: Envy

Jehovah Witnesses

Jerusalem

Jesus Christ
  See: Christ

Jew

Job
  See: Work

Joy
  See: Depression

Judging

Judgment
  God's
  and Leadership

Justice

Justification

K

Kindness
  See: Mercy

King

Kingdom

Knowing God
  Use: Christian Life

Knowledge

L

Labor
  See: Work

Lamb of God, Death of
  See: Substitution; Sacrifice

Laughter

Law
  Function of
  and Grace

Lawsuits

Laziness

Leader

Leadership
  See Service; Servanthood;
  Success

Learning
  See: Students;
  Study

Legalism
  See: Pharisee

Lent

Leprosy
  See: Pain, Gift of

Liberalism

Liberation Theology

Liberty

License

Liberty
  Christian

Lie

Life
  Happiness in
  Perspective on
  Purpose of non-
    Christian
  Uncertainty of

Lifestyle, Inconsistent
  See: Behavior, Inconsistent

Lightning

Liquor
  Use: Alcohol

Listening

Loneliness
  See: Suffering

Lord's Day

Lord's Prayer

Lord's Supper

Lordship

Love
  See: Compassion; Mercy
  Christian
  For Enemies
  God's
    Use: God, Love of
  Power of
  Romantic

Loyalty

Luck
  Use: Chance

Lust
  See: Sensuality

Lying

M

Magic

Man
  Nature of
    See: Sin

Management

Manners

Marriage
  See: Bachelor; Celibacy
  Adjustments in
  Attitudes in
  Commitment
    See: Commitment
  Communication in
  Preparation for
  Sexual Relationship
    See: Sex
  Wedding Ceremony

Masturbation

Materialism
  See: Greed; Money

Maturing
  See: Discipleship

Maturity

Meaning of Life
  Use: Life

Membership
  Use: Church, Membership

Mediocrity

Mercy
  See: Grace; Kindness

Messiah
  False Claims
  Jewish Expectation

Middle Age

Millennium

Minister
  Calling of
  Function of
  Qualities of

Ministry
  Motives for
    Use: Motives,
    for Ministry
  Qualities of
  Preparing for
  Suffering in

Miracles

Miracles of Christ

Misery
  Use: Suffering

Missionary

Missions

Mistakes
  See: Experience

Modesty

Money
  See: Covetousness; Giving;
  Greed; Materialism
  Debt
  Deceitfulness of
  Love of

Morality
  Decline of

Mormonism

Mothers
  Love for
  Praise of

Mother's Day

Motivation

Motives
  for Ministry

Movies

Murder

Music

N

Nagging

Name

Natural man

Nature of Man
  Use: Man, Nature of

Neighbor

Nervousness

Neutrality

New Man
  See: Old Man

New Year

Noise

Nostalgia

O

Oaths

Obedience
  See: Childrearing;
  Commitment; Discipline,
  Purpose of
  Reasons for

Objectives

Offerings
  See: Sacrifice

Old Man
  See: New Man

Omniscience, of God
  Use: God, Omniscience

Omnipotence of God
  Use: God, Omnipotence of

Opposition

Ordinances

Original Sin
  Use: Sin, Original

P

Pagan
  Use: Heathen

Pain
  See: Suffering

Panic
See: Fear

Parables

Parables of Christ

Paraclete
Use: Holy Spirit

Pardon
See: Salvation

Parents
See: Childrearing; Children

Passion
Motivational trait
Romantic

Passover

Past

Pastor
Use: Minister

Patience

Paul

Peace
See: Contentment; Suffering; Trials

Peer Pressure

Perfection

Persecution
of Church

Perseverance
See: Eternal Security

Persistence
See: Endurance

Perspective

Pessimism
See: Optimism

Pharisees

Philosophy

Piety

Pity

Planning

Play

Pleasure
See: Joy

Politics

Poor

Pope

Possessions
See: Materialism

Potential

Poverty

Power

Praise

Prayer
See: Lord's Prayer; Quiet Time
Answers to
Asking in Jesus' Name
Believing
Divine Guidance Through
Extent of
Importance of
Intercessory
In God's Will
Length of
Meetings
Need for
Persistence in
Power of

Relationship to Human Responsibility
Unanswered

Preachers
See: Minister

Preaching
Content
Expository
Style

Predestination
See: Salvation

Prejudice

Presuppositions

Pride

Priest
Believers as
Office of

Priorities

Problems
See: Adversity; Trials

Procrastination

Profanity
Use: Cursing

Promise

Prophecy

Propitiation
See: Expiation; Atonement

Prosperity

Prostitution
Use: Harlot
See: Adultery, Sex

Protection

Providence

Psychiatry

Psychology

Punishment
See: Childrearing; Discipline; Sin, Punishment for

Purpose, In Life
See: Life

Q

Quarreling

Quiet Time

R

Rabbi

Racism
See: Prejudice

Rage
See: Anger

Rapture

Reason

Reconciliation
See: Atonement; Forgiveness

Redemption

Regeneration
See: Conversion

Reincarnation

Relativism

Religion
   False

Religions, Compared

Repentance
See: Sorrow

Reputation
See: Integrity

Resentment

Responsibility

Rest

Restitution

Resurrection
   of Believers
   of Christ

Retirement

Retreats

Revelation
   Use:
   Bible

Revenge

Reverence

Revival

Rewards, Eternal

Rewards, Loss of

Righteousness
   Believer's
   By Faith
   National
   Personal

Ritual

Rivalry

Roles

Romance
See: Love; Marriage

Rulers

Rumor
See: Gossip

S

Sabbath

Sacrament

Sacrifice
See: Commitment; Lamb; Offering

Sadness
Use: Sorrow

Saint

Salvation
See: Faith; Forgiveness; Grace; Predestination; Propitiation; Redemption; Regeneration; Repentance; Righteousness, by Faith; Sin; Substitution
   Assurance of
   Desire for
   Gift of
   Need for
   By Works

Sanctification
See: Holiness
   Instant
   Perfectionism
   Process of

Sarcasm

Satan
See: Devil

Savior
See: Christ

Scholarship

Science

Scripture
Use: Bible

Second Coming
Use: Christ, Return of

Security

Self-control

Self-discovery

Self-discipline
Use: Discipline

Self-examination

Self-image
Use: Self-worth

Self-pity

Self-reliance

Self-righteousness

Self-sacrifice

Self-sufficiency

Self-worth

Selfishness
See: Giving, Selfishness in

Seminary

Sensuality
See: Lust

Separation

Sermon

Servant

Servanthood

Service
Disqualified for
Faithful
Motivation for
Reward of

Sex
See: Fornication;
Masturbation
Education
Sacredness of

Sheep

Sheol
Use: Hell

Shepherd
See: Minister

Sickness
See: Disease

Silence

Sin
See: Depravity;
Forgiveness; Gossip;
Holiness; Man, Nature of;
Salvation; Temptation;
Tongue; World;
Avoidance of
Confession of
Conviction of
Evidence of
Imputation of
Original
Punishment for
Struggle against
Toleration of
Unpardonable

Sinner

Skepticism

Slander
See: Gossip

Slavery

Sleep

Sluggard
See: Laziness

Social Action

Socialism

Sorrow
See: Trials

Soul-Winning
Use: Evangelism; or
Witness

Sovereignty

Speaking

Special Creation
See: Creation; Creator

Speech
See: Gossip; Tongue

Spiritual Armor

Spiritual Gifts
See: Church

Spiritual Growth
See: Christian Life;
Discipleship; Maturity

Spiritual Pride

Spiritual Warfare
See: Man, Nature of

Spring (season of)

Starvation

Steward

Stewardship
of Life
of Money
See: Giving

Students
See: Learning; Study

Stress

Stubbornness

Study

Submission
See: Marriage

Substitution

Success

Suffering
See: Discipline, Purpose of;
Pain; Peace; Trials
Reason for

Suicide

Summer (season of)

Sunday
See: Lord's Day

Suspicion

Surrender

Swearing
Use: Curse

Symbols

Sympathy

T

Tact

Talents

Taxes

Teachers
False

See: Apostate,
Example of

Teaching
See: Exhortation, Gift
of

Teamwork

Television

Temper
See: Anger

Temptation
See: Sin; Trials
Avoiding
Protection from
Resisting

Ten Commandments

Testimony
See: Witness, by Life

Testing
See: Trials
Limits of

Thankfulness
See: Gratitude; Ingratitude

Thanksgiving

Theophany

Theology

Thief

Time

Tithing
See: Giving

Tongue
See: Gossip
Control of
Results of an
Uncontrolled

Tongues

Tradition

Translations
Use: Bible, Translations

Trials
See: Discipline; Suffering
Brevity of
God's help in

Trinity

Trouble
See: Testing; Trials

Trust
Use: Faith

Trustworthiness
of God
Use: God,
Trustworthiness of

Truth

Type

U

Unbelief
See: Agnosticism; Atheism;
Doubt

Understanding

Unity
See: Church, Unity

Unpardonable Sin
Use: Sin, Unpardonable

Urim and Thumim

Ushers

V

Vacation

Valentine's Day

Values

Vanity

Victorious Living
  Use: Sanctification

Vice

Visitation

Vengeance

Virtue

Vision

Vocation
  Use: Job
  See: Work

Vow

W

Walk, Christian
  Use: Christian Life

War

Warning

Wealth
  See: Money; Stewardship
  Christian's
  Temporary nature of

Wedding
  Use: Marriage, Wedding
  Ceremony

Widow

Wife

Will
  of God
    Use: God, Will of

Wine
  Use: Alcohol

Winter (season of)

Wedding
  See: Marriage

Wisdom

Witness
  See: Evangelism
  Inconsistent

Woman
  Equality of
  Role of

Word
  of God
    Use: Bible

Work
  See: Employer; Labor

Works
  See: Salvation, by Works
  Faith, and Works;

World

Worldliness

Worry
  See: Anxiety; Fear

Worship

Wrath
  See: Anger

X

Y

Year, New
  Use: New Year

Yoke

Youth

Z

Zeal
  See: Enthusiasm

Appendix
Suggested Requirements for a Filing System Assignment

The following appendix has been written in the form of an assignment for a class. Those who are developing their filing system without the benefit of a grader's interaction could substitute a fellow minister, church secretary, or someone else who is familiar with filing and can offer insights that may improve the final product.

A. Read *Green's Filing Systems* and decide which of the two basic approaches to filing you want to use. Then decide if you will modify one of the two systems described, use a different published system, or design your own filing system. For this assignment you will prepare a file system with at least two hundred folders or add two hundred folders to an existing system. The assignment will be turned in two times (points B and C below) so that the final version can be corrected and therefore be as good as is possible.

First, Read this Book and Decide Which Approach to Filing You Want to Use

B. Complete a **first draft** of your filing system and your sermon, message, and Bible study index system. Turn them in on the date indicated on the syllabus. *Do not make up any actual file folders at this stage, only their titles.*

Second, Turn in a First Draft for Evaluation

1. The cover page of the assignment should include a general description of the file system and any factors that have influenced its development.

Include a cover page

   a. One factor that will influence your system is your future vocational plans. For example, students who do not expect to be involved in a church ministry probably will omit certain topics such as elder/ deacon qualifications, special services, DVBS, and so forth. The omission of such topics for a student intending to be a pastor would be the basis for a reduction in grade.

   b. Other factors that may influence the topics included in your system are denominational affiliation, personal interests, previous ministry experience, employment, and so forth.

2. Turn in a listing of the folders you *plan* to make up for your filing system and the number of folders listed. The grader will complete a grade sheet that will state what revisions you need to do to receive an *A* for this assignment. You can make the revisions or resubmit "as is" when the final draft is due. No grade will be recorded at this point. A resubmission is necessary for a grade to be recorded. The second submission for grade allows you to make the corrective changes noted by the grader and thus raise your grade! You can receive an *A* on the resubmission regardless of your grade on the first submission. In addition, this policy prevents many students from making up file folders that they might want to revise or relocate after they read the grader's comments.

a. Your file system must include appropriate and sufficient files for the following areas. Note that the actual location of these files will vary from student to student and will depend completely on the design of the filing system. It is not the location of the files that is the concern here, but their existence somewhere in your system.

> Files for books of the Bible (up to one hundred of the two hundred needed may be in this category)
> Files for ministry or job categories
> File(s) for correspondence (at least one folder)
> Files for other topics
> Files for theological topics
> Files for textual and topical sermons, messages, and Bible studies

b. *If you are using a separately indexed filing system* turn in the index book, or a rough draft of it. The grader may make suggestions for improvement so be sure to turn in a draft that can be written on.

c. *If you are using a topic-subtopic filing system* turn in your three-column worksheets. The worksheets do not need to be typed if they are legible. The grader may make suggestions for improvement, so be sure to turn in a draft that can be written on.

d. *If you already have a filing system* that you are revising and adding to the required two hundred folders, you must turn in a listing of the entire system. The new folders should be indicated in some manner (by a check mark or by highlighting them). Preexisting folders will not count toward the required number of new folders although they will be a factor in determining if the system is simple, consistent, and flexible.

3. Your sermon, message, and Bible study index system also must be developed. If you have never taught or preached, you may merely be deciding which system to use and thinking it through for the future. If you already have an indexing system, you may continue to use it or design a new one that better meets your needs. Your system needs to solve the potential problems discussed in chapter 5.

Include a description of your sermon-indexing system

   a. Turn in a description of your sermon, message, and Bible-study-indexing system. Remember that this is an indexing system and thus differs from where you will file these materials. Review chapter 5 if you are not clear on the difference.
   b. Be sure to describe any details the grader will need to know to understand how the index works. For example, if you decide to use the McComb system you will need to describe the following:

   > how the materials will be filed (numerically, in a special section, in the Bible section and a Topical Messages section, or in some other manner)
   > how you will make notations in the Bible (an illustration may be the easiest way to explain this)
   > where you will list topical messages (the concordance was suggested)
   > a key for any abbreviations you will use (such as BF for Bible File and TM for Topical Messages file)

C. Within two weeks of the return of your assignment to you, revise your filing system and resubmit it for a final grade. Include the original assignment, the grade sheet, and any needed changes.

Third, Turn in a Resubmission with Corrections for a Grade

   1. Often the changes can be made on the original assignment. If a new draft of the assignment is prepared, be sure to include the original assignment.
   2. Be sure to include a statement to the grader of the number of files in the final version of the assignment and a statement that the files have actually been made up and are stored in a file cabinet or box.

Student's Name:_____   Box Number:_____

File System Assignment Grade Sheet

	POINTS	
I. SIMPLE	_____	(15)
II. CONSISTENT	_____	(15)
III. FLEXIBLE	_____	(15)

IV. COMPLETE (the following areas were included)
   A. Books of the Bible files   _____   (5)

   B. Ministry or job catagory files   _____   (8)

   C. Correspondence file(s)   _____   (1)

   D. General and theological files   _____   (10)

   E. Textual and Topical Sermons, Messages and
       Bible Studies Files   _____   (3)

V. SERMONS, MESSAGES, & BIBLE STUDIES INDEX SYSTEM   _____   (8)

VI. NUMBER OF FOLDERS   _____   (20)
   Note: up to one hundred books of the Bible file folders may be
   counted toward this number.
       100 folders = 10 points
       150 folders = 15 points
       200 folders = 20 points

                                                              TOTAL_____   (100)

No grade is recorded on the first submission. You must resubmit this grade sheet, the entire assignment with any changes clearly indicated, and a statement that you have actually made the folders described in your assignment.